Social Cognition through Drama and Literature for People with Learning Disabilities

of related interest

Odyssey Now
Nicola Grove and Keith Park
ISBN 1 85302 315 9

Special Talents, Special Needs
Drama for People with Learning Disabilities
Ian McCurrach and Barbara Darnley
ISBN 1 85302 561 5

Autism
Putting Together the Pieces
Edited by John Richer and Sheila Coates
ISBN 1 85302 888 6

Disability Voice
Towards an Enabling Education
Mal Leicester
ISBN 1 85302 355 8

The Therapeutic Potential of Creative Writing
Writing Myself
Gillie Bolton
ISBN 1 85302 599 2

People Skills for Young Adults
Márianna Csóti
ISBN 1 85302 716 2

Helping People with a Learning Disability Explore Choice
Eve and Neil Jackson
ISBN 1 85302 694 8

Autism: An Inside-Out Approach
An Innovative Look at the Mechanics of 'Autism' and its Developmental 'Cousins'
Donna Williams
ISBN 1 85302 387 6

Trust and Power
Taking Care of Ourselves through Drama
Penny Casdagli
ISBN 1 85302 556 9

Making a Leap – Theatre of Empowerment
A Practical Handbook for Creative Drama Work with Young People
Sara Clifford and Anna Herrmann
ISBN 1 85302 632 8

Social Cognition through Drama and Literature for People with Learning Disabilities

Macbeth in Mind

Nicola Grove and Keith Park

Jessica Kingsley Publishers
London and Philadelphia

First published in the United Kingdom in 2001 by
Jessica Kingsley Publishers Ltd,
116 Pentonville Road,
London N1 9JB, England
and
325 Chestnut Street,
Philadelphia, PA 19106, USA.

www.jkp.com

Library of Congress Cataloging in Publication Data
A CIP catalog record for this book is available from the Library of Congress

British Library Cataloguing in Publication Data
A CIP catalogue record for this book is available from the British Library

ISBN 1 85302 908 4

Printed and Bound in Great Britain by
Athenaeum Press, Gateshead, Tyne and Wear

Contents

Acknowledgements

We would like to thank all the people who have contributed to the development of this resource through participating in workshops and discussing ideas. In particular we are grateful to the following:

Staff and pupils of Shaftesbury School, Mapledown School, Heathermount School and Meldreth Manor school.

William Sutton, Kelly Falope, Adam Butcher, Daniel Cordell, Graham Harris and Michael Fulda of Heathermount School for their lively illustrations.

Claire Rickard for providing a report and communication record sheet from the work at Meldreth Manor.

Patricia Howlin for her kind comments on an earlier draft of the manuscript.

Dave Sherratt for kindly providing access to his work, and several relevant references on play and autism.

The poem on p.93 was first printed in *Literature for All* (Grove 1998), and is reproduced by kind permission of David Fulton Publishers.

Chapter 1

Introduction

This book uses the development of social cognition as a basis for exploring Shakespeare's *Macbeth* with people who have learning difficulties. The framework and activities are flexible, and can be used across the range of ability, with individuals who have moderate, severe, or profound learning disabilities; emotional and behavioural difficulties; specific language impairments; or who are on the autistic continuum. The learning objectives for students are:

through English literature:

° to experience the atmosphere, the story line and the language of Macbeth

° to participate actively in the play, through taking roles.

These learning objectives require students to show evidence of: *affective engagement – excitement, enjoyment, alarm; anticipation, recognition and recall of the events, activities and language of the play.*

Social cognition:

° *imitation* of actions, sounds and facial expressions

° *joint attention*: looking at people and objects in the context of the play; following the direction of another person's point or gaze

° *pretence*: using objects symbolically, responding to people in role, expressing desires in role

° *mental states*: associating events and behaviour with the language of thinking and believing; experiencing gaps between appearance and reality.

This book is designed as a resource for practitioners who work with individuals with a range of learning difficulties. We begin by summarising research on the development of social cognition and describing a framework which can be used to structure work on these skills in the context of the play (Chapter 2). Chapter 3 contains a set of activities linked to the narrative of *Macbeth*, together with suggestions for introductory workshops, props and other resources. In the course of its development, the resource has been used with students with moderate learning difficulties, with autism and with profound and multiple learning difficulties, and with physical disabilities. Short case studies to illustrate the resource in practice are provided in Chapter 4. Finally, the Appendix provides an index of operational definitions of skills of social cognition, related to particular activities. This allows you to use the resource in two ways. You can select an episode, and check to see which skills it is likely to facilitate. Alternatively, you can start with the skill that you want to develop, and check in the table to select episodes that will be useful.

Chapter 2

The Development
of Social Cognition

In *Macbeth*, the narrative of external events is the simplest in any of Shakespeare's plays: Macbeth wants the crown, murders to achieve it, and is then himself unseated and killed.

Some years ago, the Royal Shakespeare Company staged a version of *Macbeth* using a bare stage with wooden walls, where the same minimal props were used in different ways in different scenes. The banqueting table, for example, where Macbeth sees the ghost of Banquo, later became the place where the Witches prepared their 'hell broth'. Several commentators at the time were taken with the idea that this production of *Macbeth* emphasised the notion that it is a drama played out inside the human mind; one in which the objects used in one scene nightmarishly transform themselves into something else for the next. The real drama of this play is internal, and is concerned with tensions between trust and betrayal, the origins and consequence of desires, the nature of appearance, and the problem of knowing what is in another person's mind. The language is charged with metaphors to do with perception and knowledge, with what seems and with what is. Macbeth himself is obsessed with the dual question of whether he can trust the evidence of his own eyes, and whether his innermost desires are evident to others. These problems are the ones that we must all solve in developing a social as well as an individual identity. They are the conundrums of a 'theory of mind'.

Many individuals with learning difficulties may find it hard to comprehend mental states, and the possible discrepancies between what people do, and what they think and feel. Although the original research on theory of mind focused on people with autism, there is now a recognition that social cognition is problematic for a range of people with learning disabilities (Park 1995; Yirmaya *et al.* 1999). Researchers have begun to identify the processes by which we discover what goes on in the minds of other people. It has been proposed that children develop a theory of mind, which involves:

- the capacity to recognise themselves and other people as beings who think

- the capacity to recognise mental states (intentions, desires and beliefs) in themselves and others, as distinct from merely experiencing such states

- the capacity to refer explicitly to their own and others' minds, and to use such concepts in explaining and predicting what they or other persons might do or say

- the capacity to recognise that there is a distinction between the real world (objective reality), and mental models of the world (subjective reality), which can lead to discrepancies between intention and action, appearance and reality, beliefs that are true and beliefs that are mistaken (Camaioni 1992; Wellman 1993).

The stages by which children develop their insights into social interactions involve a transition from perceiving and acting on the world to thinking about the world (first order representations), to thinking about the thoughts and perceptions of others (second order representations). The following brief examples also illustrate why theory of mind is sometimes described as belief-desire psychology (Baron-Cohen and Ring 1994).

First order representations derive from the child's experience of the world, gained through sensory perceptions. Many fully developed expressions of these states are to found in *Macbeth*. First, there is *I think*. Duncan trusts the thane of Cawdor; he also thinks that Macbeth is a true friend. Second, there is *I want*. Cawdor wants to be King, and later on, so does Macbeth. Evidence for the development of first order representations is found when children start to use verbs which refer to their ability to perceive, feel and think, during the second year. They first use words referring to perception (*seeing, hearing*) and feeling (*happy, sad*) before mental-state verbs such as *thinking* or *knowing*, which typically appear around the third birthday.

Second order representations involve the recognition that we can think about the mental states of others: in other words, *thinking about thinking.* For example: *I think he wants.* Banquo thinks that Macbeth wants to be King. Lady Macbeth is thinking of the mental states of others when she smears blood on the King's attendants so that other people will think they killed the King. Macbeth thinks that Duncan thinks he (Macbeth) is a true friend. This looping or recursiveness can of course lead to third order representations and beyond, becoming ever more complex: for example *I think he thinks I want –* Macbeth *thinks* that Banquo *thinks* that he (Macbeth) *wants* to be King. Awareness and understanding of other people's minds can develop a labyrinthine complexity.

The development of a theory of mind is preceded in early childhood by the development of other cognitive and emotional capacities, including:

Perception – the capacity to perceive events leads to:

Knowledge, which leads to:

Beliefs about how the world operates.

Affect – the capacity to feel and to respond to the feelings of others leads to:

Emotional states and empathy, which lead to:

the formation of *intentions or desires* and assumptions about the intentions of other people.

These capacities can be seen in operation in interactions between infants, other people, and the world around them. This book focuses specifically on processes of interaction which have been shown to be related to the development of social cognition, or theory of mind. These are:

1. Affect and imitation

2. The expression of desires and intentions

3. Joint attention to events and people in the world, which in this resource is linked to the development of knowledge and belief

4. Pretence, play and imagination.

Affect and Imitation

Infants seem programmed to view others as persons. They differentiate between objects and people, and by two months are so attuned to the emotions of others that they will copy the facial expressions of caregivers

(Haviland and Lelwica 1987). It has been suggested that imitation is one way in which empathy develops (Meltzhoff and Gopnik 1993). Imitation always involves the accommodation of one's own behaviour to that of others, and thus an implicit recognition of the connection between oneself and another person. As infants imitate the expressions of others, they come to associate feeling states with those expressions. A connection is thus established between outward state (appearance) and inner emotions.

Affective engagement seems to help to promote symbolic understanding. Bowler and Strom (1998) found that giving cues about emotional reactions helped children with autism to understand theory of mind tasks. Sherratt (1999) argues that the feelings of excitement which accompanied the activities in his programme may have stimulated the development of play behaviours in the autistic children who took part.

In this book, we deliberately seek to elicit strong emotional responses through atmospheric music and tones of voice: excitement, alarm, pleasure, and uncertainty. Participants are encouraged to imitate actions and sounds which are appropriate to the scenes.

Intentionality and Desire

Intentional behaviour is that which is directed to achieving a purpose, or goal. Infants have an innate tendency to interpret motion as involving purpose, and by nine months will distinguish between beings which can self-propel and those which cannot: i.e. between animate and inanimate. Animate entities can function as agents of action, i.e. they can move or behave independently, whereas inanimate entities can only function as objects of action. Intentionality elaborates on the concept of agency, by inferring that a mental state underlies the action: i.e. that the agent has a purpose in mind which the action is designed to fulfil (Poulin-DuBois and Shultz 1988).

How do infants come to understand that other people have intentions? The evidence suggests that children start by expressing their own desires in displays of emotion and goal-directed behaviour. During the second year, they begin to interpret the behaviour of others as indicating intentions – thus they will respond to an outstretched hand by giving an object (Masur 1983). They will also engage in teasing behaviour – pulling an object back and laughing (Reddy 1991), suggesting that they predict what someone wants, and deliberately thwart it. Passive teasing gives infants the experience of thwarted desire. When infants actively tease or joke, they are demonstrating some insight that others have expectations and desires that can be thwarted. Two-year-olds understand that people have desires, and that there are emotional consequences to achieving or failing to achieve them (Wellman 1993).

An understanding of desire and intent is fundamental to a theory of mind, which must integrate what we know and believe about the world with our predictions about the views and feelings of other people.

In this book, we focus specifically on the desire for the crown – by encouraging students to look at and reach for it, employing both teasing and pretence.

Intentional behaviour is also elicited through presenting choices: to fight with Cawdor or Duncan, between goblet and dagger (friendship or murder), flower and snake.

We discuss intentions by verbalising and signing what the characters want to happen.

With more able students, second order representations can be denoted by the use of thought bubbles to signal the difference between what people say and what they think.

Knowledge and Belief

At its simplest, knowledge represents input from the senses. Infants develop an awareness of the connections between perception, knowledge and belief – the insight that seeing, hearing, touching leads to knowing something about the world. They build up a collection of images of people, events and things that they can categorise, and use to form concepts (Mandler 1992). This in turn contributes to the formation of assumptions, or beliefs, about how things and people operate. Infants are initially egocentric – they assume that their perceptions are shared by others. Subsequently, they learn that other people see the world differently – for example, they will turn a picture round to show you, if you are sitting opposite them. Two-year-olds can judge if someone saw something or not, and the conditions under which people are able to perceive (e.g. unobstructed line of sight) (Flavell *et al.* 1981). By about four years of age, they understand that seeing leads to knowing, and that knowing leads to the formation of beliefs (Wellman 1993). It is also at this point that children begin to understand that there may be a discrepancy between *appearance* and *reality* (Astington and Gopnik 1988).

The mechanism for understanding the beliefs and perceptions of others seems to develop through *joint attention*. Young infants are intensely interested, first in faces, then increasingly in objects – but they do not seek to communicate their interest to others. However, they have an innate interest in eyes, and develop the ability to detect the direction of eye-gaze. At around 9–12 months, there is a transition to joint attention, or social referencing, when infants begin to direct their attention both to objects and people. A baby will look to an object, and look to her mother to check if she is looking in the same direction; will point out objects, and will reach to what she wants while gazing at a person to communicate a request. At this stage infants will also follow an adult's point by gazing in the same direction. Both of these behaviours (following line of regard, and alternating gaze to people and objects) suggest that infants are aware that other people attend to the world, and that their attention can be manipulated to coincide with one's own focus of interest. Joint attention seems to be a prerequisite for the development of critical functions of language: naming things and commenting on the world, as distinct from making requests (Butterworth 1991).

In this resource, understanding joint attention is elicited by encouraging participants to look at and point to objects and people, and to check the gaze of others. Perhaps more importantly, participants are encouraged to direct joint attention by *initiating* these interactions. We also note that the development of joint attention is not a social skill that is dependent upon vision. Participants who have a significant visual impairment, or who are blind, can also develop this communication skill (Perez-Pereira and Conti-Ramsden 1999). A study by Nafstad and Rodbroe (1999) includes a fascinating account of someone who is congenitally deafblind developing skills of joint attention: the person places one hand on the other person, the second hand on an object of interest, and then guides the other person's hand to that object. Both these texts illustrate the universality of similar fundamental communication skills that may often nevertheless develop in many different ways.

In the following chapters, the focus is on providing a variety of perceptual experiences that are novel and unpredictable. Appearance and reality are explicitly contrasted, by distinguishing between how characters behave and their underlying intentions – as signalled by changes in facial expression, actions that subvert ('Look behind you!') and shadow play (the dagger sequence). We make explicit use of the vocabulary associated with perception – *see, say, hear, touch, smell, taste* – and encourage students to consider what they and others perceive and do.

Pretence and Imagination

The ability to 'decouple' internal representations from real objects and events underlies the ability to engage in pretence or symbolic play, which in turn is involved in the capacity to imagine the mental state of another person and reason about it. In early shared pretence, two-year-olds seem to understand that one object can represent another, and that there is a shared attitude (intentional state) towards the symbolic use of the object. They are able to behave 'as if', but they do not necessarily conceive of other people having beliefs or imagination in respect of the object. By three, however, children seem to understand that other people have mental states – representations of the world which can be real or imaginary (Wellman 1993). Pretend play involves object substitution, which seems to grow out of (a) exploratory play with objects and (b) functional use of objects. Simile and metaphor in language grow from the perception that events in the real world have similarities to each other, and can represent the inner world of our thoughts and feelings. Developmental levels of play are outlined by Stahmer (1999), who discusses manipulative play, functional or representational play, and sociodramatic play. Manipulative play is the first type of play skill to be seen and is primarily asocial, when the child investigates objects and toys, etc. Functional or representational play skills refer to the more advanced ways in which the individual uses objects as appropriate to their canonical or social function – Stahmer cites putting a spoon to a doll's mouth as an example. Finally, sociodramatic play is described as 'an advanced form of symbolic play in which children engage in role taking and the development of a story, using object substitution and imaginary objects' (Stahmer 1999, p.33).

Although symbolic play and role play seem to pose particular difficulties for some children, notably those on the autistic continuum (Libby *et al.* 1998), research suggests that they can benefit from structured approaches to teaching play skills (Charman and Baron-Cohen 1997; Lewis and Boucher 1988; Sherratt 1999). This book addresses all three of these levels of play and seeks to provide a narrative framework with a purpose of 'social-communication guidance' (Wolfberg and Schuler 1999, p.45) to develop interactions between the individual and the physical and social environments. The starting point, for students functioning at a very early level of development, is to provide powerful contrastive experiences which we think could lead to the formation of sensory images and associations in memory. We encourage exploration and manipulation of objects within the context of formalised role play and drama. As in our previous work (*Odyssey Now*) we think of the development of symbolic play and the imagination as a transition from outer to inner experience – there is no requirement that individuals demonstrate symbolic understanding before they can participate in imaginative scenarios (Bolton 1986). Instead, we think that understanding can emerge through participation. In order to become good at dance, you have to move your body through the steps. In order to become good at imagining, you have to exercise and practise, stretching your mind in exciting, motivating and dramatic contexts.

The Language of the Play

Imaginative language is integral to poetry and drama. Here, we focus on two aspects of poetry – form, and meaning.

The *form* of poetry is its music – sound and rhythm (or in sign poetry, shapes and movements). Experimenting with form starts early – infants of course readily respond to song, and they practise different kinds of sound in their babble (Crystal 1997). Babies who are learning sign as a first language have also been observed engaging in 'manual babble', playing with different combinations of handshapes and movements (Pettito and Marentette 1991). In this resource, there are many opportunities for vocal or movement play, which we have categorised as a foundation skill in the development of imagination and play.

The *meaning* of poetic images often derives from associations between one concept and another – for example, how things appear, and how the poet feels. Poets express these in explicit comparisons (*simile*) and in the use of a term from one field of reference to describe another (*metaphor*). For example, Lady Macbeth uses a simile to rebuke Macbeth for showing his feelings too clearly in his facial expression:

> *Your face, my thane, is as a book, where men / May read strange matters.*

When Macbeth says *My way of life/Is fall'n into the sere, the yellow leaf,* he is creating a metaphoric analogy between the autumnal dying of the year and the barren ending of his own life.

Simile and metaphor grow from the perception that events and things in the real world show similarities with each other, and that they can also correspond to the events (thoughts and feelings) of our inner world. These analogies are very fundamental to the way we think and make sense of experience – we talk of people 'battling' against illness, being 'stuck in a rut', or 'over the moon' (Lakoff and Johnson 1980; Turner 1996). The beginnings of the use of figurative language can be seen in the 'over-extensions' of young children, who may apply one word to a whole range of objects which seem to share the same characteristic. For example, Melissa Bowerman's daughter learnt the word *moon* when looking at the moon, and subsequently applied it to a half grapefruit, a lemon slice, pictures of yellow and green round vegetables, and the dial on the dishwasher (Bowerman 1978). Children will also coin novel terms, or apply words in new contexts to fit gaps in their repertoire. Joseph, aged two, asked me to *dark the room* (put the light off); Ghislaine invented the words *nightieskin* (nightdress) and *frizzuring* (very cold). Sam asked if a car would become a lorry when it grew up. Children with learning difficulties can be equally creative with language: Eric, a five-year-old with Down's syndrome, used *chocolate poo-poo* as a swear word; Jayesh, aged 12, signed the compounds *red apple* for tomato and *doctor shop* for hospital. David, a young man with learning disabilities who was being bullied, said the experience was *like a dagger in my heart.* Tito, the remarkable young boy with autism featured on BBC's *Inside Story,* likened his thought processes to a black hole and described his teacher's words following him like bubbles in the wind. We should not, therefore, think that imaginative, poetic words are relevant only to students who can consciously analyse and manipulate language.

It is obvious that all activities in this book are 'pretence' – we set a boundary between the play and 'real life' by explicitly going into role at the beginning with props and costumes, and coming out of role at the end. Within the context of the play, objects are used simultaneously both functionally and symbolically – we drink from empty cups, fight with swords, and kill each other with pretend swords. We also make metaphors explicit by creating visual and tactile images to illustrate figurative language, in order to build up the sensory associations that underpin analogies between mental states and the natural world. We have used a technique of making metaphors concrete as a strategy for encouraging imaginative and creative associations. That is, we act out, or provide actual exemplars of the images, for students to explore. Discussion periods can be used with some students to talk about these associations, and tease out the basis of the imagery. You can also encourage students to create their own analogies for some of the sounds and pictures of the play.

Summary

Exploring *Macbeth* as a context for the development of these critical skills of social thinking reveals a remarkable coherence between the themes, structure and language of the play and ideas generated by contemporary research into theory of mind. The original motivation to develop the resource came from our realisation that the scene in which the Macbeths lay a false blood trail to hide their guilt has interesting similarities with the research task that has been used to explore theory of mind with autistic children. However, as we learnt more about social cognition, and explored the play in more depth, it became apparent that the parallels go far deeper. The imagery and themes of the play – eyes and seeing, facial expressions and feelings, what is said and what is unspoken, what we know of the motivation of ourselves and others – are the territory of social relationships, of moral and emotional development.

There's no art / To find the mind's construction in the face is both Duncan's dilemma and our own.

Teaching Social Cognition: Framework for Assessment and Development

We have been developing this framework through workshops we have run in schools over the past five years. In finalising the details, we have had the great benefit of reading the ground-breaking protocol developed by Howlin, Baron-Cohen and Hadwin (1999), and we have drawn substantially on their ideas. The task of linking the events of the play with the development of social cognition is a complex one, however, and our approach differs in a few key respects. In Howlin *et al.*, there are three key areas (emotion, informational states and pretend play) and five levels of development. In our book, activities are categorised into four key areas which support the development of social cognition (*affect, intention/desire, belief/knowledge* and *imagination*) at three levels: *foundation skills and experiences; early skills* and *later skills.*

○ **Foundation skills and experiences** are those which emerge in early infancy and act as the precursors to the subsequent development of theory of mind. They include affective responses, the perception of agency and expression of needs, sharing of attention and exploration of the world, and sensory, exploratory play.

○ **Early skills and experiences** are related directly to first order representations – the insight that I think and feel, and so do you. These include awareness of feelings, recognition of needs, perception of experiences, and the symbolic use of objects in play.

○ **Later skills and experiences** lead to second order representations: the recognition that emotions are related to desires and beliefs; the recognition of the distinction between true beliefs and false beliefs, pretend play and the imagination. There is more explicit awareness of the feelings, intentions and beliefs of other people.

Table 2.1 shows the four key areas of activities at the three levels of social cognition.

Table 2.1 Dimensions of social cognition at three levels of development				
	Affect	**Desire and Intent**	**Belief and Knowledge**	**Imagination and Play**
Foundation	Affective responses Imitation Expressing feelings	Attention to agents Goal-directed behaviour Pre-verbal expression of wants Passive teasing	Attention to objects and events Mutual gaze Joint attention Gaze monitoring Declaratives Active teasing	Sensory images Object exploration and manipulation Object gestures Play with sounds and movements Role play conventions
Early	Awareness of feelings Situation/feeling connection Stock reactions Basic emotion vocabulary	Expression of desire and intent Awareness of wants of others Cause and effect Desire vocabulary	Naming and description Recognition of actions of self and others Perspective taking Perception vocabulary Belief vocabulary	Symbolic use of objects Pretend actions Role play Figurative language
Later	Recognition of feelings of others Psychological causality Mixed feelings Complex emotion vocabulary	Recognition of intentions of others Intention/action connection Explanations	Recognition of beliefs of others Perception/ knowledge/belief connection Appearance/ reality distinction Explanations Mental state vocabulary False belief False belief vocabulary	Role adoption Recognition of imaginative states Imagination vocabulary Figurative language

Chapter 3

Activities

Introduction

The play has been divided into seven episodes, with some transposition of events and scenes when this makes for a more logical and simpler adaptation. Within each episode there are several activities which are linked to the plot and dialogue of the play to move the story on. Each activity can be used to develop or apply a range of skills of social cognition – *affect, desire, belief* and *imagination* – at different levels: *foundation skills, early skills* and *later skills*. Some activities have a very specific focus at a particular level, such as false belief, a later-emerging aspect of theory of mind which comes into the category of perception-belief. Other activities have more general purposes. Sometimes an activity may involve different categories at different levels. For example, students who have developed higher levels of social cognition may be able to perceive and discuss the affective implications of an activity, whereas for students at an earlier level, the emphasis may be more on mutual engagement, or symbolic play. Nearly all the activities involve basic affective experiences and participation in role play, but not all tap every level, or every dimension of social cognition. You may also want to develop different activities and skills from the ones we have identified. A description of the behaviours we are looking for, cross-referenced to relevant activities, can be found in the Appendix.

Questions

Discussion points are marked by questions, which encourage everyone to reflect on what is said, done, thought and felt. Questions should be used with students who are able to articulate ideas and respond, in speech, signs, or through communication boards. For students operating at foundation levels, or at very early, one-word levels, you may want to concentrate more on visual attention, by asking 'What' or 'Where' questions to encourage looking and pointing.

The questions we have identified operate at two levels. The early level of social cognition relates to evident desires, feelings and perceptions. Later levels relate to more complex emotions, and conflicts between desires, beliefs and feelings. You can make the questions simpler by providing a choice between visual alternatives, such as the think, feel, say bubbles with symbol representations, or pictures. You do not have to ask all the questions – this would go on for ever! So be selective, thinking about the skills that you want as the focus of the activity. Also watch the timing of questions – sometimes it may be appropriate to freeze the action, and have a discussion, for example, if students are becoming over-excited, or conversely, bored. At other times, however, you may have created a special atmosphere that you don't want to destroy, so it may be better to leave discussion to the end. For example, we have not included a question session immediately after Macbeth's death, in Episode 7. We should not be so obsessed with assessing what students know that we intervene too early, and deprive them of the opportunity to soak up experience over time, and build their understanding through apprehension and familiarity.

Issues of Appropriateness

Macbeth is an incredibly powerful play, and we have not attempted to disguise the violent intentions and actions of the protagonists. Our experience is that people with learning difficulties find the play just as cathartic as anyone else does. However, you may be working with students who have obsessive interests or anxieties about things such as blood, knives, and darkness. For these students, you may feel it is appropriate to omit activities (e.g. the dagger play) or downplay some scenes. For example, we felt unable to dramatise the murder of Lady Macduff and her children in any way that seemed acceptable, and so we have left it out. (You may be more creative than we are, and if you can find a way of doing it that is not stomach-turning, do reinstate it!) We have found that it is possible to do scenes in quite a low key way, which maintains interest and attention, but does not lead to students becoming over-excited or upset (see the case studies in the Appendix).

Poetic Language – Working with Quotations

The actual language of the play is used wherever it seems appropriate, and quotations are printed in italic. You can, of course, substitute other quotations, or expand or omit sections. The text can either be programmed onto a communication aid, such as a Big Mac (a simple communication device which is especially good for dialogue) or you can simply read it out as an accompaniment to the action.

Ongoing Commentary

In order to develop skills of social cognition, we think students with learning difficulties need plenty of very explicit exposure to the language of mental states, in contexts which are heightened for them. The suggested activities offer opportunities to develop several key skills, and these can be highlighted by your commentary, using terms such as *see, hear, think, know, feel.* For example, in the numerous games which are based on 'Grandmother's Footsteps' (see Duncan's arrival at the castle; Banquo's murder) you can say 'Banquo, look, look behind you! Oh no, he didn't see them! We can see the murderers creeping up, but Banquo didn't!'

Cultural and Religious Issues

The use of witches, ghosts and prophecy as vehicles for exploring Macbeth's surrender to the evil forces within him may be unacceptable to some religious or cultural groups. It's important to remember that their function in the play is highly symbolic. However, all texts are the property of the audience as well as the writer, and you must feel free to adapt the resource in any way that seems appropriate. Shakespeare took huge liberties with his own source material, after all.

Beginnings

Warm-up activities may be helpful for some groups. These can be used to familiarise students with some of the techniques we have used to bring the text alive, and to make links with the teaching of social cognition. The following activities recur throughout our adaptation, and can be practised beforehand.

Co-operative Games

Simple physical exercises that involve co-operation and reliance on each other can be used to demonstrate concepts of trust and friendship, and can be found in most books of drama games (see e.g. Jennings 1986). Bear in mind, however, that what happens in *Macbeth* is that trust is undermined and betrayed – so you will need to make very firm boundaries between the trust built up between individual students who play these games, and what happens in the context of the play. For example, if you play a co-operative game in 1.2, to demonstrate the King's belief that Cawdor is his friend, you will need explicitly to come out of role and talk about how we are friends and can trust each other – 'Let's see what happens to the King and his friends'.

Figure 3.1 Examples of convention 'bubbles'

Think, Feel, Say, Look Conventions

You can use cartoon 'bubbles' held on sticks (see Figure 3.1). Talk about how we see with our eyes, talk with our mouths, feel in our hearts, show feelings on our faces, think with our minds. Sometimes what we see and think and feel are the same, and sometimes they are different. Play some matching games with the bubbles – happy face, cross thought, etc.

Mind's Eye

These activities can be used to explore the way we can recreate things in our imagination. Play 'Kim's Game', or other visual memory games – look at something, then hide it, and try to describe it from memory. Students close their eyes or turn round, and then say who is sitting next to them. Talk about how we dream when we are asleep, and have really vivid experiences.

Actions and Gestures

Bowing, greeting, drinking, looking, pointing, reaching.

Character Workshop

You may want to have particular props or sounds to symbolise the main characters. Talk about the characters' attributes, and find ways of indicating who they are. For example, a drum for Macbeth (taken from his warlike character and the line *A drum, a drum, Macbeth doth come*); a bell for Duncan (to signify the religious nature of kingship, and the bell which sounds just before his murder), a vocalised 'ahh' sound for Lady Macbeth, which can start out triumphant, but turn into a cry of despair.

Ideas for Starting Sessions

Bring the students into a circle. Put the props in the middle, and decide who is taking which roles.

Use some of the character noises – a drum, a bell, a cry – as your starting point.

Use the three witches to introduce each episode. You can do this as a whole group, with some of the questions and answers programmed onto a voice output communication aid. Alternatively, students can take it in turns to act these roles. To increase the atmosphere, you can add in some musical effects and trail gauzy fabric to suggest cobwebs.

Witch 1   *When shall we three meet again*

   In thunder, lightning or in rain?

Witch 2   *When the hurly-burly's done*

   When the battle's lost and won.

Witch 3   *That shall be ere set of sun.*

Witch 1.	*Where the place?*
Witch 2	*Upon the heath.*
Witch 3	*There to meet with Macbeth.*
All witches	*Fair is foul and foul is fair!*
	Hover through the fog and filthy air.

Endings

It is important to provide a space for students to make the transition between the drama and real life, especially when working with a play as forceful as this. We have used the standard technique of a FINISH cue – sound or visual image, and then bringing everyone into a circle to 'de-role' by putting all the props used in the session into a basket in the middle. Playing quiet music while looking at a candle is a good way of moving from the darkness of the play into the light of day.

The Story: Macbeth Act I Scenes I–4

The King of Scotland is Duncan. He has two loyal thanes, Cawdor and Macbeth. Cawdor plots to obtain the crown, and declares war on Duncan. He is defeated in battle, and his titles are given to Macbeth.

EPISODE I. Battle Royal

Resources

Gold crown
Silver crown
Mounting block
Think/say/feel bubbles.

1.1. Welcome the King

The King comes in wearing a golden crown. Everyone bows and says 'Hail King Duncan!' as Duncan moves round the circle, touching hands. Shake hands, hug, high fives, swing people.

Think bubble	FRIENDS
Feel bubble	HAPPY
Say bubble	FRIENDS

SOCIAL COGNITION

Foundation Skills

Affect	Affective responses. Imitation. Expressing feelings – affection, pleasure.
Desire	Attention to agents. Goal-directed behaviour.
Belief	Mutual gaze. Gaze monitoring.
Imagination	Role-play conventions

Early Skills

Affect	Awareness of feelings. Situation/feeling connection. Stock reactions. Basic emotion vocabulary.
Belief	Naming.
Imagination	Pretend actions. Role play.

1.2. King of the Castle

Duncan (big golden crown) stands next to and higher than Cawdor (silver crown) on different levels (e.g. on PE equipment). Direct attention to each in turn, using spotlight or torch.

Give a deep bow for Duncan, a small bow for Cawdor. Prompt Cawdor to look and/or reach towards Duncan's crown.

Duncan turns to Cawdor and says 'You are my friend.'

Cawdor says 'Yes, friend' (holding think bubble).

At this point you might like to play some trust games.

Think bubbles	Cawdor: WANT + CROWN; Duncan: FRIEND.
Say bubbles	Cawdor: FRIEND; Duncan: FRIEND.

QUESTIONS

EARLY SKILLS	LATER SKILLS
Who is the King?	
Who is most important?	
What does Cawdor say?	
	What does Cawdor think?
	What does Cawdor want?

Michael

QUESTIONS

SOCIAL COGNITION

Foundation Skills

Desire	Attention to agents. Goal-directed behaviour. Expression of wants. Attention to objects. Joint attention.
Belief	Attention to objects/events. Joint attention. Gaze monitoring. Declaratives.
Imagination	Role-play conventions.

Early Skills

Desire	Expression of desire and intent. Awareness of wants of others. Desire vocabulary.
Belief	Naming. Perspective taking – others. Perception vocabulary.
Imagination	Role play.

Later Skills

Feeling	Psychological causality: desire-emotion, belief-emotion. Understanding and use of complex emotions – jealousy. Recognition of feelings of others.
Desire	Recognition of intentions of others. Explanations.
Belief	Recognition of beliefs of others. Perception-belief/knowledge connection. Appearance/reality distinction; Mental-state vocabulary. False belief. False belief vocabulary.
Imagination	Role adoption.

1.3. The Golden Round

Everyone stands or sits in a close circle. Encourage them to look at or reach for the golden crown. Tease by bringing the crown within reach, then moving it away. Verbalise for them – 'Yes, we really want the crown, we'd like to be King but no (headshake), King Duncan is my friend, he trusts me.'

When we get to Cawdor, he decides he does want the crown, and moves out of the circle.

Cawdor persuades people to come over to his side – beckons others, says/signs COME.

Students look between Cawdor and Duncan. Can they choose where to go?

QUESTIONS

EARLY SKILLS	LATER SKILLS
Who is the King?	
	Who wants to be King, but isn't?
	Why does Cawdor want to be King?
Who do you want to be with, the King or Cawdor?	

SOCIAL COGNITION

Foundation Skills

Affect	Affective responses. Imitation. Expression of feelings – excitement, alarm.
Desire	Attention to agents. Goal-directed behaviour. Expression of wants. Desire vocabulary.
Belief	Attention to objects. Joint attention. Mutual gaze. Gaze monitoring. Declaratives. Teasing (passive).
Imagination	Sensory images. Role-play conventions.

Early Skills

Affect	Awareness of feelings. Stock reactions.
Desire	Expression of desire, choice and intent. Awareness of wants of others. Cause and effect.
Belief	Naming. Perspective taking – self and others.
Imagination	Role play.

Later Skills

Feeling	Recognition of feelings of others. Psychological causality. Complex emotions – greed, jealousy. Mixed emotions.
Desire	Recognition of intentions of others. Intention/action connection. Explanations.

Belief	Recognition of beliefs of others. Perception-belief/knowledge connection. Appearance/reality distinction. Mental-state vocabulary. False belief. False belief vocabulary.
Imagination	Role adoption.

1.4. Battle Royal

Two lines are drawn up for the two opposing sides. Duncan has the golden crown. His supporters form a barrier to repulse Cawdor and Cawdor and his supporters attempt to reach Duncan and the crown.

Use theme music or chant war cries – Duncan is the King; Cawdor for King. Cawdor's music gets quieter as he is beaten back.

Cawdor is surrounded and captured. His crown is taken to give to Macbeth, and he is led away.

What he has lost, noble Macbeth has won.

There's no art

To find the mind's construction in the face

He was a gentleman on whom I built

An absolute trust

Duncan says: 'I trust you, Macbeth, I trust you Banquo, I trust you, Malcolm, I trust you Donalbain.'

Play some trust games.

Crown Macbeth with Cawdor's silver crown and put him on the next level to Duncan.

Spotlight on Macbeth and Duncan. Everybody bow.

Duncan says: 'Macbeth, you are my friend. You have the silver crown. I will come to dinner with you.'

Think bubble	FRIEND
Say bubble	FRIEND
Feel bubbles	HAPPY/SAD

QUESTIONS

EARLY SKILLS	LATER SKILLS
Where is the King? Where is Cawdor?	
Who has the silver crown?	
Who wants the gold crown?	
What did Cawdor/King/Macbeth do?	
What does the King say? (friend)	What does the King think? (friend)
What does Macbeth say? (friend)	What does Macbeth think? (kill)
	How do the King and Macbeth feel?
	How does Cawdor feel?

SOCIAL COGNITION

Foundation Skills

Affect	Affective responses. Imitation. Expression of feelings – excitement, fear.
Desire	Attention to agents. Goal-directed behaviour. Expression of wants.
Belief	Gaze monitoring.
Imagination	Play with sounds. Role-play conventions.

Early Skills

Affect	Awareness of feelings. Situation/feeling connection. Emotion vocabulary – fear, anger, pleasure, affection.
Desire	Expression of desire, choice and intent. Awareness of intents of others. Cause and effect.

Belief   Naming. Recognition of actions of self/others. Perspective taking – self and others.

Imagination Role play.

Later Skills

Feeling   Recognition of feelings of others. Psychological causality. Complex emotions – jealousy. Understanding of mixed emotions.

Desire   Recognition of intentions of others. Intention/action connection. Explanations.

Belief   Recognition of beliefs of others. Perception-belief/knowledge connection. Appearance/reality distinction. Mental-state vocabulary. False belief. False belief vocabulary.

Imagination Role adoption.

Michael

Michael

EPISODE 2. Heath and home

The Story: Macbeth Act I Scenes 3–5

> Macbeth meets the witches, who prophesy that he will be King. He returns home and discusses the forthcoming visit of Duncan with his wife.

Resources

> Gold crown, silver crown, copper crown
>
> Torch
>
> Daggers
>
> The 'blanket of the dark' – a black cloth with star shapes cut out of it
>
> Mask which has a smiling face on one side and an angry face on the other
>
> Plastic snake
>
> Artificial flower.

2.1. Weird Sisters

The witches appear.

Where are the witches? Students reach, point or look towards the witches.

The witches dance, chanting words from the play:

> *The weird sisters hand in hand*
>
> *Thus do go about about*
>
> *Thrice to thine and thrice to mine*
>
> *And thrice again to make up nine.*

or:

> *Fair is foul and foul is fair*
>
> *Hover through the fog and filthy air.*

Circle dance. All move round one way three times, then in the opposite direction three times. Make sounds, and hand movements. Or they circle around the spectators, until a drum is heard.

> *A drum, a drum*
>
> *Macbeth doth come.*

Macbeth and Banquo enter from one corner of the hall. They move forward to a drumbeat, played by one or two students. After the drumbeat, they stop – and everyone has to look and point in their direction.

QUESTIONS

EARLY SKILLS	LATER SKILLS
Who is coming?	
Ask the witches – who do you see?	
Ask others – who do the witches see?	
Ask Macbeth and Banquo – who do you see?	
Macbeth and Banquo ask: *What are these, So wither'd and so wild in their attire?* (i.e. witches)	Do the witches seem to know Macbeth? Does Macbeth know the witches? Which words in the text tell us that the witches do know Macbeth, but he does not know them?

SOCIAL COGNITION

Foundation Skills

Affect   Affective responses. Imitation. Expressing feelings – fear and excitement.

Desire   Attention to agents. Goal-directed behaviour.

Belief   Attention to events (sound location). Joint attention. Gaze monitoring. Declaratives.

Imagination Sensory images. Sound and movement play. Role-play conventions.

Early Skills

Belief   Naming. Perspective taking – self and others. Perception vocabulary. Belief vocabulary.

Imagination   Role play. Figurative language.

Later Skills

> **Belief**   Recognition of beliefs of others. Explanations. Mental-state vocabulary.
>
> **Imagination**   Role adoption.

2.2. King Hereafter

Each witch offers Macbeth a crown, looking at him as they do so. Macbeth reaches to each crown.

Or: Only Duncan's crown is used. The witches hold the crown out to Macbeth, who reaches for it.

> **Witches**   *All hail Macbeth,*
>
> *All hail Macbeth, thane of Cawdor*
>
> *All hail Macbeth, who shall be king hereafter*

The witches move slowly away. Macbeth and Banquo look after them. You can make a rushing sound, like the wind, as they go.

Look and point as the witches disappear.

> *Whither are they vanished?*
>
> *Into the air, and what seemed corporal*
>
> *Melted, as breath into the wind.*

SOCIAL COGNITION

Foundation Skills

> **Affect**   Imitation.
>
> **Desire**   Attention to agents. Goal-directed behaviour. Pre-verbal expression of wants.
>
> **Belief**   Attention to objects. Mutual gaze. Joint attention. Gaze monitoring. Declaratives.
>
> **Imagination**   Object exploration and manipulation. Play with sound. Role-play conventions.

Early Skills

Desire	Expression of desire and intent. Awareness of intentions of others. Desire vocabulary.
Belief	Naming. Perspective taking – self and others. Perception and belief vocabulary – gone, see.
Imagination	Role play.

Later Skills

Desire	Recognition of intentions of others.
Imagination	Role adoption.

2.3. My Black and Deep Desires

Bring Duncan in, wearing his golden crown, to stand next to Macbeth. Shine a torch on each.

> *Signs of nobleness, like stars shall shine*
>
> *On all beholders*

Students look at and point to each in turn.

Using daggers and torches, go round the group. Shine the torch on each person in turn while he or she holds the dagger at eye level and is prompted to make stabbing movements. Say the following lines as you switch off the torch quickly, and move the hand down out of vision – or over the eyes.

> *Stars, hide your fires*
>
> *Let not night see my black and deep desires*
>
> *The eye wink at the hand*
>
> *Come, thick night*
>
> *And pall thee in the dunnest smoke of hell*
>
> *That my keen knife see not the wound it makes*
>
> *Nor heaven peep through the blanket of the dark*
>
> *To cry 'Hold, hold'.*

Alternatively, you could create star images which can be used at other points in the play, perhaps by cutting star shapes out of a black cloth and shining torches behind them, or covering the torch itself with a star template. To hide the fires of the stars, simply switch off the torch, and cover the dagger with the cloth.

QUESTIONS

EARLY SKILLS	LATER SKILLS
Which one is the King?	
What did the witches tell Macbeth?	
	What do the witches think will happen?
	What does Macbeth think?
	How does Macbeth feel?
	What does Macbeth want to do?
Which words go with dark?	Why is the dark like a blanket?
	What is Macbeth's black and deep desire?
	Why does he want the stars to hide their fires/be put out?

SOCIAL COGNITION

Foundation Skills

Desire	Attention to agents. Teasing (passive).
Belief	Attention to objects/patterns. Joint attention.
Imagination	Sensory images. Object manipulation. Object gestures.

Early Skills

Desire	Awareness of wants of others. Desire vocabulary.
Belief	Naming.
Imagination	Symbolic use of objects. Figurative language.

Later Skills

Affect	Recognition of feelings of others. Psychological causality: desire–emotion, belief–emotion. Mixed feelings. Complex emotion vocabulary.
Desire	Recognition of intentions of others. Intention/action connection. Explanations.
Belief	Recognition of beliefs of others. Mental-state vocabulary.
Imagination	Imagination vocabulary. Figurative language.

2.4. The Letter

You can use the preceding questions as the basis for constructing the letter which Macbeth writes to Lady Macbeth. In it he tells her:

° how he met the witches

° what the witches said

° that he is coming home to see her.

This is an exercise in perspective taking, since in order to decide the content of the letter we have to recognise that Lady Macbeth does not know what we know, or what Macbeth knows.

You can choose whether or not to say anything more explicit about Macbeth's desires and intentions at this point. In the play, his intentions only become really focused through his interactions with his wife – and even then he vacillates.

Project the letter, in whatever text is appropriate (e.g. symbols, pictures of the witches and a crown, words) for the students to read on an overhead slide, or write the letter together, fold it up and give it to Lady Macbeth to read out. For students using objects of reference, give a relevant object associated with the witches, and pass it around, saying 'we met the witches'.

SOCIAL COGNITION

Foundation Skills

Belief	Attention to objects/patterns.
Imagination	Object manipulation.

Early Skills

Belief	Naming. Recognition of actions of self/others. Perspective taking – self and others.
Imagination	Symbolic use of objects. Pretend actions; Role play.

Later Skills

Belief	Recognition of beliefs of others. Mental-state vocabulary. Description of events.
Desire	Recognition of intentions of others. Intention/action connection. Explanations.
Imagination	Imaginative play. Role adoption.

2.5. Homecoming

Announce the arrival of Macbeth with a drumbeat. Lady Macbeth and Macbeth advance to meet each other, making welcoming gestures.

The following dialogue can be programmed onto communication aids. Alternatively, two members of staff can stand behind each character and voice-over for them.

Half the group can act as Macbeth, half as Lady Macbeth, or individuals can take the roles.

Macbeth	*My dearest love*
	Duncan comes here tonight
Lady Macbeth	*And when goes hence?*
Macbeth	*Tomorrow as he purposes*
Everybody shouts	*NO!*
Lady Macbeth	*Oh never shall sun that morrow see.*
	Your face, my lord is as a book wherein one may read strange matters.
	To beguile the time, look like the time itself
	Suppose the innocent flower
	But be the serpent under it. He that's coming Must be provided for …

QUESTIONS

EARLY SKILLS	LATER SKILLS
What are they saying?	
	What are they thinking?
	What are they going to do?

SOCIAL COGNITION

Foundation Skills

Affect	Affective responses. Imitation. Expressing feelings – affection/welcome.
Belief	Mutual gaze. Joint attention. Gaze monitoring.
Imagination	Role-play conventions.

Early Skills

Affect	Recognition of feelings. Situation/feeling connection (welcome).
Belief	Perception vocabulary.
Desire	Awareness of wants of self/others.
Imagination	Symbolic use of objects. Figurative language. Role play.

Later Skills

Affect	Recognition of feelings of others. Psychological causality. Mixed feelings. Complex emotion vocabulary.
Belief	Recognition of beliefs of others. Mental-state vocabulary.
Desire	Recognition of intentions of others. Intention/action connection. Explanations.
Imagination	Imagination vocabulary. Figurative language.

2.6. Looking Fair, Feeling Foul

For students functioning at an early or foundation level, try using masks, fair one side, foul the other. Reverse these, encouraging students to look. Students can try the masks on themselves, and look in a mirror, or can look at another person wearing a mask. Imitate happy and sad or angry faces. Copy the facial expression of a student, to reflect feelings back to them.

For students functioning at later levels, try changing your face by smiling, then dragging your hand over your face and then frowning. Encourage students to take on different facial expressions, looking in a mirror. Have students in pairs, facing then back to back like a Janus face – one smiling, one frowning. Turn round so that the audience can see the different faces. Discuss how feelings are shown in facial expressions, and how one person may experience a range of emotions simultaneously.

Present a flower, then bring up the snake, and make it 'bite' each student. Present snake and flower for choice. Look like the innocent flower – but be the serpent under it. Discuss how a face might look like a flower, and what this would represent; how a face might look like a snake, and what this would mean. Can you change your face from a 'flower' to a 'serpent'? Discuss how it is possible to pretend – using a facial expression to express one kind of feeling – whilst really feeling something else.

Look and Feel bubbles can be used to express this discrepancy.

SOCIAL COGNITION

Foundation Skills

Affect	Affective responses. Imitation. Expressing feelings.
Desire	Attention to agents. Teasing (passive).
Belief	Attention to objects/patterns. Mutual gaze. Joint attention. Gaze monitoring. Declaratives.
Imagination	Sensory images. Object manipulation.

Early Skills

Affect	Recognition of feelings. Basic emotion vocabulary.
Imagination	Symbolic use of objects. Imaginary objects. Figurative language.

Later Skills

Affect	Recognition of feelings of others. Psychological causality. Mixed feelings. Complex emotion vocabulary.
Belief	Recognition of beliefs of others. Appearance/reality distinction. Mental-state vocabulary. Perception-belief/knowledge connection. False belief. False belief vocabulary.
Imagination	Imagination vocabulary. Figurative language.

EPISODE 3. Daggers of the Mind

The Story: Macbeth Act 1 Scene 6 – Act 2 Scene 3

Duncan arrives to stay at Macbeth's castle, and is welcomed by the Macbeths. That night, during the feast, they argue about whether or not to murder him. After the feast, Duncan retires to bed for the night.

Resources

Two tapes, or Big Macs, with birdsong and raven croaks
Think/look/feel bubbles
Goblet
Daggers (plastic, cardboard, metal knife).

3.1. Ravens and Martlets

Duncan and his retinue arrive at Macbeth's castle. Is this a safe, or a hostile place? Position Duncan and his group at one side of the room, and the Macbeths at the other. Each group takes a few steps forwards in turn, and as they do so, either sweet birdsong, or a raven's sinister croaking is played, accompanied by the appropriate text.

Duncan	*This castle hath a pleasant seat; the air*
	Nimbly and sweetly recommends itself
	Unto our gentle senses.
	This guest of summer
	The temple haunting martlet, does approve

> *By his loved mansionry that the heaven's breath*
>
> *Smells wooingly here.*

Lady Macbeth *The raven himself is hoarse*

> *That croaks the fatal entrance of Duncan*
>
> *Under my battlements.*

Finally, the two groups meet. All bow to Duncan, who goes around the group touching hands (as in 1.1, Welcome the King).

QUESTIONS

EARLY SKILLS	LATER SKILLS
What does Duncan hear as he approaches the castle?	
What does Lady Macbeth hear as Duncan approaches?	
	What does Duncan think of the castle, and why?
	Do you think the castle is a nice, safe place? Why/why not?
	The raven is a bird which is often seen in stories when something bad is about to happen. What does Lady Macbeth mean when she talks of the raven croaking as Duncan enters the castle?

SOCIAL COGNITION

Foundation Skills

Affect	Affective responses.
Desire	Attention to agents. Goal-directed behaviour.
Belief	Attention to sounds.
Imagination	Sensory images.

Early Skills

    Affect   Affective responses. Stock reactions.

    Belief   Naming. Recognition of actions of others. Perspective taking – self/others. Perception vocabulary.

    Imagination Figurative language.

Later Skills

    Belief   Recognition of beliefs of others. Perception/knowledge connection. Explanations. Mental-state vocabulary. Appearance/reality distinction. False belief. False belief vocabulary.

    Imagination Figurative language.

3.2. Light and Dark

This activity dramatises the debate between the Macbeths.

For students functioning at early developmental levels, make the choice very explicit. Duncan with his crown stands in front of a student, whose hands or arms are held by two staff members, one on each side. The student is pulled first towards the 'light' as one of the appropriate lines is said, then towards the 'dark', when an opposing line is said. Repeat a few times, with groups on each side joining in. Then stop, and present the student with a goblet (on the 'light' side, for friendship) and a dagger (on the dark side, for murder). Whichever one the student looks at or touches represents the choice made for one side of the argument or the other.

Repeat with another pair of lines, for the next student, until all have made a choice.

For students who are more aware of the role play (i.e. that Duncan does not know that this argument is taking place), you could place Duncan's crown in front of the student, rather than having him there in person.

Another way of dramatising the decision, if you have access to a darkened room and a good lighting system, is to use dark and light areas. Two people stand on either side, whispering lines, and alternately pulling the student first to the light, then to the dark.

LIGHT	DARK
His virtues plead like angels	*Vaulting ambition*
Tears shall drown the wind	*Be so much more the man*
So clear in his great office	*When you durst do it, then you were a man*
He's here in double trust	*Screw your courage to the sticking place*
Kinsman and guest	*Unguarded Duncan*
Shut the door	*Bear the knife*
I dare not	*I would*
Golden opinions	*Our great quell*
If we should fail	*We'll not fail*
We will proceed no further in this business	*I am settled*

QUESTIONS

EARLY SKILLS	LATER SKILLS
Who wants the goblet? Who wants the dagger?	What does Macbeth want to do?
	What does Lady Macbeth want to do?
	Who wins the argument, and why?

Think and feel bubbles

Macbeth:　　　　KILL THE KING? NO!

Lady Macbeth:　KILL THE KING? YES!

SOCIAL COGNITION

Foundation Skills

Affect	Affective responses. Imitation.
Desire	Goal-directed behaviour. Pre-verbal expression of wants. Teasing (passive).
Belief	Attention to objects/patterns. Joint attention.
Imagination	Sensory images. Object manipulation.

Early Skills

Desire	Expression of desire and intent. Awareness of wants of others. Desire vocabulary.
Imagination	Symbolic use of objects. Figurative language.

Later Skills

Affect	Recognition of feelings of others. Psychological causality: desire–emotion, belief–emotion. Mixed feelings. Complex emotion vocabulary – love, loyalty, greed, ambition.
Desire	Recognition of intents of others. Intention/action connection. Explanations.
Imagination	Role adoption. Imagination vocabulary. Figurative language.

3.3. Honoured Hostess

Everyone is given a 'drink' – to symbolise the feast. Then it is time for Duncan to retire. Lady Macbeth offers him her hand to conduct him up to bed. Macbeth tiptoes behind Duncan with the dagger. When Duncan looks round, he puts the knife behind him and smiles. This is a good opportunity for doing the pantomime favourite 'Look behind you!' A staff member may need to act as Macbeth here, or support the student who is taking this role.

Duncan is led to a chair or bed, and left to sleep.

Think bubbles

Duncan: FRIEND; Macbeths: KILL

QUESTIONS

EARLY SKILLS	LATER SKILLS
What does the King see?	
What is the King doing?	What does the King think and feel about Macbeth? Is he right?
	What do the Macbeths think and feel? Are they really friendly?
	There's something the King doesn't know – but we do. What is it?

Duncan *sees* the Macbeths being friendly. He is *happy* because he is visiting people he *thinks and trusts* are his friends. He does *not know* that the Macbeths plan to kill him.

SOCIAL COGNITION

Foundation Skills

Affect	Affective responses. Imitation. Expressing feelings.
Desire	Attention to agents. Teasing (passive).
Belief	Attention to objects/patterns. Mutual gaze. Joint attention. Gaze monitoring. Declaratives. Teasing (active).
Imagination	Object manipulation. Object gestures. Role-play conventions.

Early Skills

Affect	Awareness of feelings. Situation/feeling connection. Stock reactions. Basic emotion vocabulary – happiness, fear and excitement.
Desire	Expression of desire and intent. Awareness of wants of others.
Belief	Naming. Recognition of actions of self/others. Perspective taking – self and others. Perception vocabulary.
Imagination	Symbolic use of objects. Role play. Figurative language.

Later Skills

Affect	Recognition of feelings of others. Psychological causality.
Desire	Recognition of intentions of others. Intention/action connection. Explanations.
Belief	Recognition of beliefs of others. Explanations. Mental-state vocabulary. Perception-belief/knowledge connection. Appearance/reality distinction. False belief. False belief vocabulary.
Imagination	Role adoption.

3.4. Dagger Play

This activity dramatises the guilt which leads Macbeth to his waking dream of a dagger leading him to Duncan's murder.

You can first play a very simplified 'Kim's Game', either in the whole group or small groups. Put a dagger in the middle of the group, and then cover it up. Ask students what is there, and to describe it – how big, what colour, what shape, how they would hold it.

Contrast the feel of a real dagger (knife), a plastic dagger, a cardboard dagger; a picture of a dagger; a shadow dagger.

Project the shadow of a dagger onto the wall or ceiling, and encourage students to reach for it. As they do so, read the text:

> *Is this a dagger which I see before me*
>
> *The handle toward my hand? Come, let me clutch thee:*
>
> *I have thee not, and yet I see thee still.*
>
> *Art thou not, fatal vision, sensible*
>
> *To feeling as to sight? Or art thou but*
>
> *A dagger of the mind, a false creation*
>
> *Proceeding from the heat-oppressed brain?*

Then you can work in pairs, one staff member and one student (or with able students, two students paired up). Hold the dagger in front of the student, who can lay their hand on it, or just look. Follow the dagger where it leads (to Duncan).

> *Thou marshall'st me the way that I was going*
>
> *And such an instrument I was to use*
>
> *The bell invites me*

Finish the activity by sounding the bell, and all saying together:

Hear it not, Duncan, for it is a knell

Which summons thee to heaven or to hell.

Sound a bell – encourage students to move towards the sound. This is best done with the whole group, because otherwise it is too distracting.

QUESTIONS

EARLY SKILLS	LATER SKILLS
What can you see?	
What did the dagger look like?	
What is Macbeth looking at?	Is it a real dagger that Macbeth sees?
	Why is Macbeth so sure he is looking at a dagger?
	How can we see things that aren't there?

We can make pictures in our minds of things that we know about, even if they aren't in front of us. When we dream, we are imagining things. In 'Kim's Game', we can imagine what things look like, and it helps us to remember them.

SOCIAL COGNITION

Foundation Skills

Belief   Attention to objects/patterns. Joint attention. Gaze monitoring. Declaratives.

Imagination Sensory images. Object manipulation.

Early Skills

Belief   Naming and description. Perspective taking – self and others. Perception vocabulary. Belief vocabulary.

Imagination	Symbolic use of objects. Imaginary objects. Figurative language.

Later Skills

Belief	Appearance/reality distinction. Recognition of beliefs of others. Mental-state vocabulary. Perception-belief/knowledge connection. False belief. False belief vocabulary.
Imagination	Recognition of imaginative states. Imaginative play. Imagination vocabulary. Figurative language.

EPISODE 4. The King is Dead, Long Live the King

The Story: Macbeth Act 2 Scene 2 – Act 2 Scene 3.

In the middle of the night, the Macbeths creep to Duncan's chamber and Macbeth stabs him. Lady Macbeth has earlier drugged the guards, and now she smears their faces with blood and puts daggers in their hands. The Macbeths are overcome with the horror of what they have done, and are startled to hear a knocking on the castle gate announcing the arrival of Banquo and the King's two sons. They wash their hands to get rid of the blood, and Macbeth kills the guards to silence them. Everyone suspects that Macbeth is the murderer, but he is appointed King in Duncan's place. The two princes escape to England.

Resources

Daggers
Sheet to cover Duncan
'Blood'-red ribbon/material, face paint
Bowl of water, cloth
Gold crown
Think/feel/say bubbles.

4.1. Hear Not My Steps

You can introduce this scene by reading the following text, very spookily. Note that the rhythm of the piece, with punctuation on the half lines, suggests Macbeth's fear and hesitation. You can dramatise this by moving alternately forward and taking steps back, each time there is a pause or a comma (this can be done as a whole-group activity).

> *Now o'er the one half world*
>
> *Nature seems dead, and wicked dreams abuse*
>
> *The curtain'd sleep; now witchcraft celebrates*
>
> *Pale Hecate's offering and wither'd murder*
>
> *Alarum'd by his sentinel, the wolf*
>
> *Whose howl's his watch, thus with his stealthy pace*
>
> *With Tarquin's ravishing strides, towards his design*
>
> *Moves like a ghost. – Thou sure and firm-set earth*
>
> *Hear not my steps, which way they walk, for fear*
>
> *The very stones prate of my whereabout*
>
> *And take the present horror from the time*
>
> *Which now suits with it. I go and it is done.*
>
> (a bell rings)
>
> *The bell invites me. Hear it not, Duncan, for it is a knell*
>
> *Which summons thee to heaven or to hell.*

Feel bubble

FRIGHTENED.

QUESTIONS

EARLY SKILLS	LATER SKILLS
What is Macbeth doing?	
What does Macbeth hear?	
	How does Macbeth feel?

	Why is he feeling like this?
	What frightening words does he use to tell us how he feels?
	What does he imagine the bells and the stones are saying to him?

SOCIAL COGNITION

Foundation Skills

Affect	Affective responses. Imitation. Expressing feelings – fear, excitement.
Belief	Attention to events – sound location.
Imagination	Sensory images.

Early Skills

Affect	Awareness of feelings. Situation/feeling connection. Basic emotion vocabulary.
Belief	Recognition of actions of others. Perspective taking – others.
Imagination	Figurative language.

Later Skills

Affect	Recognition of feelings of others. Psychological causality.
Desire	Intention/action connection. Recognition of intentions of others. Explanations.
Imagination	Imaginative play. Role adoption. Recognition of imaginative states. Imagination vocabulary.

4.2. Every Noise Appals Me

Duncan is asleep in his chamber, guarded by a servant who is asleep, and covered by a white sheet. Macbeth and Lady Macbeth take their daggers, and creep towards him.

Ask the students to think of noises they might hear at night – owl, creaking door, footsteps, wind, fox barking. For people who cannot vocalise, or imitate noises, provide appropriate sound-making instruments. Divide everyone into groups, and give each group a noise. Macbeth and Lady Macbeth start at one end of the room, moving towards Duncan, keeping very quiet. Each group in turn makes a noise, at which the Macbeths must stop in their tracks. Then they move on again.

The following text can be read halfway through the activity.

Macbeth	*Didst thou not hear a noise?*
Lady M	*I heard the owl scream and the crickets cry.*
	Did not you speak?
Macbeth	*When?*
Lady M	*Now.*
Macbeth	*As I descended?*
Lady M	*Ay.*
Macbeth	*How is't with me, when every noise appals me?*

SOCIAL COGNITION

Foundation Skills

Affect	Affective responses. Imitation. Expressing feelings.
Desire	Attention to agents. Goal-directed behaviour.
Belief	Attention to event – sound location. Joint attention. Gaze monitoring.
Imagination	Sensory images. Sound play. Role-play conventions.

Early Skills

Affect	Awareness of feelings. Situation/feeling connection. Stock reactions. Basic emotion vocabulary.
Belief	Naming. Perspective taking – self and others' hearing. Perception vocabulary.
Imagination	Sensory images. Pretend actions.

Later Skills

Belief	Recognition of beliefs of others. Mental-state vocabulary.
Imagination	Role adoption.

4.3. Murder Most Foul

At last Macbeth reaches the bedroom where the King sleeps – opens the door, creeps quietly up to the sleeping man, and stabs him …

Unroll red ribbons, or a long length of red material, fixed with Velcro or safety pin to Duncan. The trail should end at the Macbeths (you can fix one end to one of them if you like). Encourage students to track the trail, either through gaze or touch.

Who would have thought the old man to have so much blood in him?

Have red face paint and a bowl of water ready. Put red paint on the hands of Macbeth and Lady Macbeth. Hold up their hands to show what has happened; go round the group to show them. Put red hands onto the sheet to make bloody prints.

This scene can be done in a low-key way if students are likely to be frightened – for example, by putting a hand on the King rather than using a pretend dagger; or by putting red paint only on the hands of staff.

QUESTIONS

EARLY SKILLS	LATER SKILLS
What has happened?	
Who has killed the King?	
	How do we know?
	Why have the Macbeths killed the King?

SOCIAL COGNITION

Foundation Skills

Affect	Affective responses. Expressing feelings.
Desire	Attention to agents. Goal-directed behaviour.
Belief	Attention to objects/events. Joint attention. Gaze monitoring. Declaratives.
Imagination	Sensory images. Role-play conventions.

Early Skills

Affect	Awareness of feelings. Situation/feeling connection. Stock reactions.
Desire	Cause and effect.
Belief	Naming. Recognition of actions.
Imagination	Pretend actions. Role play.

Later Skills

Desire	Recognition of intents of others. Intention/action connection. Explanations.
Belief	Perception-belief/knowledge connection. Explanations.
Imagination	Imaginative play. Role adoption.

4.4. Knock Knock

Make a loud knocking noise. Say to the group: 'Someone's at the door. What can we do? Quick!' This is a time for some quickfire discussion.

QUESTIONS

EARLY SKILLS	LATER SKILLS
Who has killed the King?	
	Who is at the door?
	What can we do to hide the evidence?

Lady Macbeth   *A little water clears us of this deed.*

Go get some water

And wash this filthy witness from your hand.

Smear red paint onto the servant's hands, and give the dagger to the servant (this can be a staff member if students are reluctant to take the role). Move the blood trail (ribbon or material) to the servants. Come back and wash hands as the knocking goes on.

An alternative scenario is that everyone in the group is given bloody hands, and then washes them frantically as the knocking goes on.

The porter scene is the original 'knock knock' joke, and you might like to include a few here, if you want to break the tension, though we find it works better to carry straight on.

Malcolm, Banquo and Macduff come in, to find the King is dead. Everyone holds up their hands in turn. They have to work out who has killed the King, by following the trail of blood; looking at everyone's hands, and the faces of the servants; finding the daggers.

Discuss whether or not they are correct, and how you know.

QUESTIONS

EARLY SKILLS	LATER SKILLS
Where are the daggers?	
Whose hands are dirty, and whose hands are clean?	
What did the Macbeths do?	Why have they washed their hands? Why have the Macbeths put blood on the hands of the servant, and given him the dagger?
What do Malcolm and Macduff see?	
Who has really killed the King?	Who do they think has killed the King?
	Why do they think this?
Who is sad?	How do they feel now that their King is dead? How do the Macbeths feel?

Malcolm, Banquo and Macduff *see* that the servants have blood on their hands, and are holding the daggers. They do *not see* blood on the Macbeths. So they *think* that the servants have killed the King. They do *not know* that the Macbeths did it, and then washed their hands. The Macbeths *seem* innocent, but *really* they are guilty.

> *Those of his chamber, as it seem'd, had done't.*
>
> *Their hands and faces were all badged with blood,*
>
> *So were their daggers which, unwiped, we found*
>
> *Upon their pillows.*

SOCIAL COGNITION

Foundation Skills

Affect	Affective responses. Imitation. Expressing feelings.
Desire	Attention to agents. Goal-directed behaviour.
Belief	Attention to objects/patterns. Joint attention. Gaze monitoring. Declaratives.
Imagination	Sensorimotor exploration. Role-play conventions.

Early Skills

Affect	Awareness of feelings. Situation/feeling connection. Stock reactions. Basic emotion vocabulary.
Desire	Cause and effect.
Belief	Naming. Recognition of actions of others. Perspective taking – recognition of what self/others see. Perception vocabulary. Belief vocabulary.
Imagination	Pretend actions. Role play.

Later Skills

Affect	Recognition of feelings of others. Psychological causality.
Belief	Appearance/reality distinction. Recognition of beliefs of others. Explanations. Mental-state vocabulary. Perception-belief/knowledge connection. False belief. False belief vocabulary.
Imagination	Role adoption.

4.5. Long Live the King

The servant is taken to prison (or murdered by Macbeth if you want to stick closely to the narrative). Who can become King now that Duncan is dead? Hold up the crown, and invite people to choose a successor by pointing, or saying their name. The sovereignty must fall on Macbeth. Some people cheer, others boo and hiss. Put gold crowns on Macbeth and Lady Macbeth. Bow and curtsy, as the new King and Queen move past. Everyone says 'Congratulations' or 'Long live the King'. Point to the King and Queen. You can use a crown and robes that are too big for Macbeth, to symbolise the fact that he is not really big enough/good enough to be King. This anticipates the metaphor of the title hanging on him, which is used in the final act.

QUESTIONS

EARLY SKILLS	LATER SKILLS
Who should be the King?	Who wants to be King?
Who is the King now? Who is the Queen?	
What is everyone saying?	
	What is everyone thinking? (Macbeth, Lady Macbeth, people in the crowd, the servant in prison.)

Write the ideas in the think bubbles, and hold them up. A mural can be created on the wall, by drawing an outline around volunteers from the audience, and sticking 'their' think bubble above the outline.

SOCIAL COGNITION

Foundation Skills

Affect	Imitation.
Desire	Attention to agents. Goal-directed behaviour.
Belief	Joint attention. Gaze monitoring.
Imagination	Role-play conventions.

Early Skills

Affect	Stock reactions.
Desire	Expression of intent – choice making. Awareness of wants of others.
Belief	Naming. Perspective taking – others (say). Perception vocabulary – say.
Imagination	Role play.

Later Skills

Desire	Recognition of intentions of others. Intention/action connection. Explanations.

Belief   Recognition of beliefs of others. Appearance/reality
                   distinction. Mental-state vocabulary.

Imagination Role adoption.

EPISODE 5. Spectre at the Feast

> *The Story: Macbeth Act 3 Scene 1 – Act 3 Scene 4*
>
> Macbeth is made King, but he does not feel secure in his kingship.
> He knows that Banquo and others suspect that it was he who
> murdered Duncan. He begins systematically to eliminate his
> enemies. He invites Banquo to a great feast, but organises his ambush
> and killing in the forest. At the feast, however, he sees Banquo's
> ghost taking his place at the table. He is overcome with horror, and
> breaks down. The guests leave in disarray.

Resources

Goblets, plates, cutlery, for feast
Large piece of black card (enough for the outline of a complete silhouette
of Banquo's body)
Chalk to mark the position of Banquo's body.

5.1. Killer

Say to the group:

Macbeth and Lady Macbeth were King and Queen but they were not
happy. They knew everyone suspected they had murdered King
Duncan and they felt guilty. Macbeth killed anyone he thought he
could not trust. People began to whisper about Macbeth. This is what
they whispered (speak very quietly):

Macbeth, Macbeth, Macbeth hath murdered sleep.

If Macbeth hears you, or sees you signing, you're dead. Stop when he
turns round.

Macbeth stands with his back to the group. He must look round quickly,
and indicate the person he wants to kill. The victim should 'die'. This can
be done in several ways, depending on the ability level and sensitivity of
the people concerned:

- ° Act it (as dramatically as you like!)
- ° Move out of the acting space to the side, so that the group gets smaller and smaller
- ° Cover the victim with a light, transparent black veil
- ° Have a pretend axe or sword, and strike the victim on the shoulder
- ° Put pressure on someone's shoulder.

SOCIAL COGNITION

Foundation Skills

Affect	Affective responses. Imitation. Expression of feelings – fear, excitement.
Desire	Attention to agents. Teasing (passive).
Belief	Attention to events (novelty). Mutual gaze. Joint attention. Gaze monitoring. Declaratives. Teasing (active) (Macbeth actor).
Imagination	Role-play conventions.

Early Skills

Affect	Awareness of feelings. Situation/feeling connection. Stock reactions.
Desire	Expression of intent. Cause and effect.
Belief	Naming. Recognition of actions of others. Perspective taking – self and others (see). Perception vocabulary.
Imagination	Role play.

Later Skills

Affect	Recognition of feelings of others. Psychological causality. Complex emotion vocabulary – suspicion.
Desire	Recognition of intents of others. Intention/action connection.
Belief	Appearance/reality distinction. Mental-state vocabulary. False belief. False belief vocabulary.
Imagination	Role adoption.

5.2. Fears Stick Deep

Banquo and Macbeth stand back to back, come forward in turn and speak to the audience. Banquo says:

> *Thou hast it now, King, Cawdor, Glamis, all*
>
> *As the weird women promised, and I fear*
>
> *Thou played most foully for it.*

He holds up a think bubble, with the message MACBETH KILLED THE KING and/or a feel bubble with the message FRIGHTENED.

Macbeth says:

> *To be thus is nothing,*
>
> *But to be safely thus. Our fears in Banquo*
>
> *Stick deep...*

He holds up a feel bubble with the message FRIGHTENED.

For students functioning at early levels, Macbeth and Banquo can stand opposite each other. They alternately turn towards each other saying 'Friend' or 'Yes' and away from each other saying 'Foe' or 'No'.

Students functioning at later levels may be able to engage in more discussion. Macbeth and Banquo turn to each other, and say 'You are my friend'. Hold up the say bubbles, each with the message FRIEND.

Hold up the feel and say bubbles at the same time. Discuss whether Macbeth and Banquo can in fact trust each other.

Point to/look at Macbeth and Banquo.

QUESTIONS

EARLY SKILLS	LATER SKILLS
Which one is Macbeth? Which one is Banquo?	
What do Macbeth and Banquo say to each other?	
	What does Banquo think about Macbeth?
	What does Macbeth think about Banquo?

	What does Macbeth think that Banquo thinks about the murder of Duncan?
	How does Macbeth feel about Banquo?
	Is Macbeth really Banquo's friend?
	Should Banquo trust Macbeth?
	What might Macbeth do, and why?

Macbeth and Banquo *say* they *trust* each other. However, Banquo *thinks* that Macbeth murdered King Duncan, and Macbeth *thinks* that Banquo *thinks* that he was the murderer. Macbeth is *afraid* of Banquo.

SOCIAL COGNITION

Foundation Skills

Affect	Affective responses. Imitation.
Desire	Attention to agents.
Belief	Mutual gaze. Joint attention.

Early Skills

Affect	Awareness of feelings. Situation/feeling connection. Basic emotion vocabulary.
Belief	Perspective taking – others. Perception vocabulary.
Imagination	Role play. Figurative language.

Later Skills

Affect	Recognition of feelings of others. Psychological causality. Complex emotion vocabulary.
Desire	Recognition of intentions of others. Intention/action connection. Explanations.
Belief	Recognition of beliefs of others. Appearance/reality distinction. Mental-state vocabulary. False belief. False belief vocabulary.
Imagination	Role adoption.

5.3. Light Thickens

Macbeth asks Banquo to come and have dinner with him. Banquo agrees, but says he is going out for a ride in the forest beforehand. You can act this dialogue first in simple speech and signing, and then use the actual text, which may be recorded onto communication aids.

Macbeth	*Tonight we hold a solemn supper, sir*
	And I'll request your presence.
	Ride you this afternoon?
Banquo	*Ay, my good lord*
Macbeth	*Is't far you ride?*
Banquo	*As far, my lord, as will fill up the time*
	'Twixt this and supper.
Macbeth	*Fail not our feast.*
Banquo	*My lord, I will not.*

Banquo leaves, and Macbeth plans his murder. As the following speech is read, gradually darken the room, to the accompaniment of birds croaking, and the flapping of wings.

Macbeth	*Come, seeling night*
	Scarf up the tender eye of pitiful day
	And with thy bloody and invisible hand
	Cancel and tear to pieces that great bond
	Which makes me pale. Light thickens
	And the crow makes wing to the rooky wood;
	Good things of day begin to droop and drowse,
	Whiles night's black agents to their preys do rouse.

Note that if you are going to use method 3 for the appearance of his ghost later in this episode, Banquo will need to wear some clearly identifiable costume, such as a plastic helmet and brightly coloured cloak. Banquo starts to walk down the room (you can do this along a line of 'trees', if you like, which Macbeth hides behind). Macbeth follows him. Every so often, Banquo hears a footstep, or a twig crack, looks round, but sees nobody – Macbeth freezes or hides behind trees. You can do the 'Look behind you' routine. Provide a commentary, saying 'What can Banquo hear? What can he see? He's feeling frightened.'

Eventually Macbeth catches up with Banquo, and stabs him, so that he falls on the floor, onto a large piece of black card (you will need to staple several sheets together). Draw a chalk outline around his body. Banquo can stay in position while questions are asked.

QUESTIONS

EARLY SKILLS	LATER SKILLS
Where is Banquo?	
What has happened to him?	
Who killed Banquo?	Why did Macbeth kill Banquo?
Which words in the speech make you think of darkness and night?	Macbeth wants the night to come quickly why?

SOCIAL COGNITION

Foundation Skills

Affect Affective responses. Imitation. Expression of feelings.

Desire Attention to agents. Goal-directed behaviour.

Belief Joint attention. Gaze monitoring. Declaratives.

Imagination Sensory images. Role-play conventions.

Early Skills

Affect Awareness of feelings. Situation/feeling connection. Stock reactions. Basic emotion vocabulary.

Desire Cause and effect.

Belief Naming. Recognition of actions. Perspective taking – recognition of what others see. Perception vocabulary.

Imagination Role play. Figurative language.

Later Skills

Affect   Recognition of feelings of others. Psychological causality.

Desire   Recognition of intentions of others. Intention/action connection. Explanations.

Belief   Recognition of beliefs of others. Mental-state vocabulary. Explanations.

Imagination   Role adoption. Figurative language.

5.4. Fail Not Our Feast

Lay the table (count how many places are needed). Make sure there is a place for Banquo. Lady Macbeth and Macbeth welcome their guests, and everybody sits down, and starts to eat and drink and enjoy themselves. There is a prominent empty chair for Banquo.

Macbeth asks: 'Where is Banquo? I hope he is coming, I hope nothing's happened to him.'

Banquo's ghost appears at the feast but only Macbeth can see him. There are various alternative ways of playing this.

° Macbeth is seated slightly away from the others, looking towards Banquo's ghost (the outline). Everyone turns their back, except for Macbeth. Banquo's ghost is raised up so that Macbeth can see it, and he must point to it and shout its name. As everyone turns round, the outline is laid flat on the floor again. Everyone says: 'No, Banquo is not here. It's a chair/stool.'

° The next method uses an actual Banquo, perhaps with white face paint and/or a sheet to denote ghostly status. Someone at one end of the table proposes a toast, and while everyone is looking in one direction, Banquo appears next to Macbeth, and then quickly disappears again. Macbeth then tells everyone to look at Banquo, and they shake their heads and say, 'No, there's no one there, it's only a stool.'

° The third method relies on the association of Banquo with a particular piece of costume. The guests pass the costume to one another, to the accompaniment of music, singing and drinking. At a signal, there is silence, and whoever is holding the costume puts it on. Macbeth looks and points and says 'It's Banquo' and the person wearing the costume denies this, and says his or her own name.

This game is repeated four or five times, until Macbeth calls out:

Thou canst not say I did it; never shake

Thy gory locks at me.

Macbeth and Lady Macbeth then shout and gesture to everyone to go away.

Lady Macbeth says:

This is the very painting of your fear

Why do you make such faces? When all's done

You look but on a stool.

QUESTIONS

EARLY SKILLS	LATER SKILLS
Where is Banquo?	
Who sees Banquo?	
	Who does not see Banquo?
	What does Macbeth think he sees?
What do the guests/Lady Macbeth see?	
	Is Banquo really at the feast?
	Can Macbeth really see Banquo, or is he imagining it?
	How does Macbeth feel about the murder of Banquo?

SOCIAL COGNITION

Foundation Skills

Affect   Affective responses. Imitation. Expression of feelings.

Desire   Attention to agents. Teasing (passive).

Belief	Attention to objects/patterns. Joint attention. Gaze monitoring. Declaratives. Teasing (active).
Imagination	Object gestures. Role-play conventions.

Early Skills

Affect	Awareness of feelings. Situation/feeling connection. Stock reactions.
Belief	Naming. Perspective taking – self and others. Perception vocabulary. Belief vocabulary.
Imagination	Pretend actions. Role play.

Later Skills

Affect	Recognition of feelings of others. Psychological causality: emotion (guilt) leading to belief.
Belief	Appearance/reality distinction. Recognition of beliefs of others. Explanations. Mental-state vocabulary. Perception-belief/knowledge connection.
Imagination	Role adoption. Understanding of imaginative states. Imaginative language.

EPISODE 6. Shadow Play

The Story: Macbeth Act 4 Scene 1

Macbeth is tormented by fear that he will lose his crown. He visits the witches again, and they provide him with insights into his future. They promise him that he will never be defeated unless Birnam Wood comes to Dunsinane castle. Secure in the knowledge that woods do not move, Macbeth returns to his castle.

Resources

Cauldron

Horrid feely things to put in: plastic snakes, spiders and frogs, joke eyeballs, fingers etc.

Giant wooden spoon

Drum

Cress seeds and two pots

Masks or puppets

Crown.

6.1. Witches' Brew

Everyone sits in a group around the cauldron. Each person puts in a contribution to the witches' brew, and stirs it. The items can be taken out of a bag, which is passed round, or chosen from the centre. Students can be encouraged to reach for an object they would like to put in. Everyone recites the charm, swaying to the rhythm:

> *Round about the cauldron go*
>
> *In the poisoned entrails throw*
>
> *Toad that under cold stone*
>
> *Days and nights has thirty-one*
>
> *Sweltered venom sleeping got*
>
> *Boil thou first i' th' charmed pot.*

Refrain   *Double, double, toil and trouble*

Fire burn and cauldron bubble.

Fillet of a fenny snake

In the cauldron boil and bake:

Eye of newt and toe of frog

Wool of bat and tongue of dog

For a charm of powerful trouble

Like a hell-broth, boil and bubble.

Refrain *Double, double, toil and trouble*

Fire burn and cauldron bubble.

Take it in turns to stir the cauldron in pairs, looking into the contents and at each other.

Alternatives: Create a less spooky brew by using common objects, such as plastic foods, to practise naming. In this case, you will have to change the words of the poem. (It won't be so much fun, either!)

With students who function at later levels, you can imagine all the ingredients. Each person is passed the cauldron, and thinks of something horrid to put in. Then everyone chants the refrain. The poem can be extended by students creating their own images and rhymes.

QUESTIONS

EARLY SKILLS	LATER SKILLS
What's this?	
What do you want to put in the cauldron?	What might the witches put in the cauldron?
What is in the cauldron now?	
What did you/others put in the cauldron?	

SOCIAL COGNITION

Foundation Skills

Affect	Affective responses. Imitation. Expression of feelings: enjoyment, disgust.
Desire	Goal-directed behaviour. Expression of intent.
Belief	Attention to objects. Mutual gaze. Joint attention. Gaze monitoring. Declaratives. Teasing (active).
Imagination	Sensory images. Object exploration and manipulation. Sound/movement play. Role-play conventions.

Early Skills

Affect	Awareness of feelings. Situation/feeling connection. Stock reactions.
Desire	Expression of desire. Awareness of wants of others. Desire vocabulary.
Belief	Naming. Awareness of actions of others. Perspective taking – self/others. Perception vocabulary.
Imagination	Symbolic use of objects. Pretend objects. Role play. Figurative language.

Later Skills

Imagination	Role adoption. Figurative language.

6.2. By the Pricking of My Thumbs

Use a drum to herald the arrival of Macbeth. Everyone says together:

> *By the pricking of my thumbs*
> *Something wicked this way comes.*

This can be prolonged – sound the drum, then pause, then say the verse, then pause again. Repeat three or four times, getting louder each time.

Macbeth knocks on the door and comes in. Everyone points to him – you can say together: *All hail Macbeth, that shall be King hereafter.*

Macbeth	*How now, you secret, black and midnight hags* *What is't you do?*
Witches	*A deed without a name.*

(You can encourage more able students to improvise their own answers here.)

EARLY SKILLS	LATER SKILLS
Who is this?	
Who can Macbeth see?	Why has Macbeth come to see the witches?
Who can the witches see?	

SOCIAL COGNITION

Foundation Skills

Affect	Imitation.
Desire	Attention to agents.
Belief	Attention to events. Joint attention. Gaze monitoring. Declaratives.
Imagination	Sensory images.

Early Skills

Belief	Naming. Perspective taking – self/others. Perception vocabulary.
Imagination	Role play.

6.3. The Seeds of Time

Macbeth	*If you can look into the seeds of time*
	And say which grain will grow, and which will not
	Speak to me.
Witches	*Speak. Demand. We'll answer.*

(Note: this speech has been transposed from Banquo in Act 1 Scene 3.)

Make this metaphor concrete by sowing some cress seeds in two pots. Ask the students to predict which will grow and which will not. Use this to explain that we do not know what the future holds. The 'seeds of time' can be revisited each day during the course of the project. (Note: you will need to do some behind the scenes doctoring to ensure that some grow and others wither.)

SOCIAL COGNITION

Foundation Skills

> **Belief** Attention to objects. Joint attention.
>
> **Imagination** Sensory images. Object exploration and manipulation.

Early Skills and Later Skills

> **Imagination** Figurative language.

6.4. Shadow Play

The witches show Macbeth the future in a series of apparitions. These are:

1. An armed head (i.e. helmeted) to represent Macduff.

   Macbeth, Macbeth, Macbeth, beware Macduff!

2. A blood-covered infant, representing Macduff, who was born by Caesarian section, and thus technically not 'born of woman'. The apparition of course also represents Macduff's murdered children, and (if you believe some theories) the child to whom the Macbeths refer at times, who seems to have died in infancy.

   Macbeth, Macbeth, Macbeth

   Be bloody, bold and resolute; laugh to scorn

   The power of man, for none of woman born

   Shall harm Macbeth.

3. A child crowned with a tree in his hand.

   Macbeth shall never vanquished be until

   Great Birnam Wood to high Dunsinane hill

   Shall come against him.

   Macbeth asks if Banquo's children will inherit the crown, and is shown a procession of kings (*will the line stretch out to the crack of doom?*).

Use masks, puppets or shadow puppets to create one or more of these illusions (you may want to omit the blood-covered child).

At its simplest, one person can walk around the group, wearing the crown and a mask. This is the king who will come. Students can be encouraged to reach and touch the masks, puppets or shadows, making sounds as they do so.

SOCIAL COGNITION

Foundation Skills

Belief	Attention to objects/patterns. Mutual gaze. Joint attention. Gaze monitoring.
Imagination	Sensory images. Object exploration. Sound play.

Early Skills

Belief	Naming. Perspective taking – self.
Imagination	Figurative language.

Later Skills

Imagination	Figurative language.

6.5. Fortune Telling

This is a pair activity, in which one person is the witch and the other Macbeth. Open the hand out and trace over the lines on the palm – this is effectively a hand massage experience. Play spooky music as you do this.

SOCIAL COGNITION

Foundation Skills

Belief	Mutual gaze. Joint attention.
Imagination	Sensory images.

6.6. Vanishing Trick

Macbeth	*Where are they? Gone?*
	Saw you the weird sisters?
Lennox	*No my lord.*
Macbeth	*Came they not by you?*
Lennox	*No, indeed my lord.*

This can be done as a group activity or in pairs.

Group activity: Macbeth sits in the middle of the group, or opposite. The witches move past him and vanish back to their places or behind a screen. Macbeth looks after them as they go, first in one direction then in another.

Pairs: Macbeth sits, witch stands opposite.
To engage attention:

° trail a long piece of material across Macbeth's cheek, so that he turns his head

° make a sound from the direction of the next witch to leave

° start close to Macbeth and move slowly away backwards, holding eye gaze all the time.

Alternative: Macbeth hides his eyes. The witches disappear, but leave clues as to where they have gone (e.g. trail of toes, eyes, fingers or just footprints). Macbeth has to work out which direction they went.

SOCIAL COGNITION

Foundation Skills

Desire	Attention to agents. Teasing (passive).
Belief	Attention to events. Mutual gaze. Joint attention. Gaze monitoring. Declaratives. Teasing (active).

Early Skills

Belief	Naming. Perspective taking – self and others. Perception vocabulary. Belief vocabulary.

Later Skills

Belief	Perception/knowledge connection. Explanations. Mental-state vocabulary.

EPISODE 7. Out, Out, Brief Candle

The Story: Macbeth Act 5 Scenes 1–9

Macbeth and Lady Macbeth are obsessed by their guilt. Lady Macbeth walks in her sleep and relives the murder of Duncan. She then kills herself. Duncan's son, Malcom, is gathering allies as he advances on Dunsinane castle. He disguises his advancing troops by telling them to cut branches of the trees of Birnam Wood, and carry them as they march.

Resources

Candle or torch
Large crown
Large cloak
Red face paint
Tree branches (real or pretend).

7.1. Sleep No More

Sleep, or the lack of it, is a key theme in the play. Duncan is killed whilst he is sleeping, and after the murder, the Macbeths lose the ability to sleep peacefully; this culminates in Lady Macbeth's sleepwalking scene. There are many beautiful images and descriptions of sleep and its value to us. This game contrasts the peace and healing nature of sleep with the guilty wakefulness of the Macbeths.

Macbeth and Lady Macbeth sit or lie in the middle of a circle of people. Make sure everyone is comfortable and relaxed. Darken the room if possible, with one small light or candle available. Play very gentle music – such as a lullaby. Use one or more of the following lines of text from the play to soothe everyone, saying them rhythmically and emphasising the soft 's' sounds.

The innocent sleep

Sleep that knits up the ravelled sleeve of care

Sore labour's bath

Balm of hurt minds

Great nature's second course

Chief nourisher in life's feast.

Then use one or more of the lines of text below to disturb the sleep of the Macbeths. There are several ways of doing this:

- ° Different people say different lines, starting quietly and working up to a crescendo, so that the voices are coming from all sides.

- ° Whisper the lines close to the Macbeths.

- ° Say one of the lines really loudly and suddenly to wake them up (this is only to be recommended with students who can tolerate loud, sudden noises).

- ° Use musical instruments – a drum or a bell to wake them.

> *One cried 'Murder!'*
>
> *Macbeth does murder sleep*
>
> *Sleep no more: Macbeth shall sleep no more*

The Macbeths can toss and turn and sit bolt upright as they wake. Then they lie down, and the game starts again.

QUESTIONS

EARLY SKILLS	LATER SKILLS
Who is sleeping?	
Who is not sleeping?	
What can they hear?	
	Why can't they sleep?
	What are they dreaming of?

SOCIAL COGNITION

Foundation Skills

Affect	Affective responses. Imitation. Expressing feelings – calm and anxiety.
Desire	Attention to agents.
Belief	Attention to events (sound location). Joint attention. Gaze monitoring.
Imagination	Sensory images. Play with sounds.

Early Skills

Affect	Awareness of feelings. Situation/feeling connection.
Belief	Recognition of actions of others. Perspective taking – self and others. Perception vocabulary.
Imagination	Figurative language.

Later Skills

Affect	Recognition of feelings of others. Psychological causality. Complex emotion vocabulary.
Imagination	Understanding of imaginative states. Imagination vocabulary.

7.2. Sleepwalking

Lady Macbeth cannot stop thinking about the murder, and she walks in her sleep.

Talk about dreams. Lie down on the floor – pretend to go to sleep; what are you thinking of?

Darken the room, except for a lighted candle or torch. Students move quietly about the room, as Lady Macbeth's monologue is spoken.

One person acts as Lady Macbeth, holding the light, walking backwards and beckoning. The partner must follow, looking at the light. Read extracts from her speech:

> *Who would have thought the old man to have so much blood in him?*

> *What, will these hands ne'er be clean?*

> *Here's the smell of the blood still.*

Wash your hands put on your nightgown. I tell you yet again, Banquo's buried; he cannot come out on's grave.

Come, come, come, come, give me your hand.

What's done cannot be undone.

To bed, to bed, to bed.

Blow out the candle, or switch off the torch to represent her death. Stay in the dark for a moment, while someone says:

God, God, forgive us all.

The Queen my lord is dead.

She should have died hereafter

There would have been a time for such a word.

Play a clip of sad music, and encourage students to vocalise a cry of sorrow. (*What is that noise? It is the cry of women, good my lord.*)

QUESTIONS

EARLY SKILLS	LATER SKILLS
What is Lady Macbeth doing?	Why is Lady Macbeth walking in her sleep?
	What is she remembering?
	Why does she need a light?
	Why does she keep washing her hands?
	How does she feel about what has happened?

SOCIAL COGNITION

Foundation Skills

Affect	Affective responses. Expressing feelings – sadness.
Desire	Attention to agents.

Belief	Attention to objects. Mutual gaze. Joint attention. Gaze monitoring.
Imagination	Sensory images. Play with sounds.

Early Skills

Affect	Awareness of feelings. Situation/feeling connection. Basic emotion vocabulary.
Belief	Recognition of actions of others.
Imagination	Role play. Figurative language.

Later Skills

Affect	Recognition of feelings of others. Psychological causality. Complex emotion vocabulary.
Imagination	Role adoption. Understanding of imaginative states. Imagination vocabulary.

7.3. Revolting Tyrant

Macbeth stands at one end of the room, wearing a crown and a cloak which are too big for him, and with red face paint on his hands. (You can use a puppet or painted outline for this, if it is not appropriate for students or staff to take the role.)

Malcolm stands at the other end of the room and points to Macbeth, saying:

> *Now does he feel*
>
> *His secret murders sticking on his hands*
>
>
> *Now does he feel his title*
>
> *Hang loose upon him, like a giant's robe*
>
> *Upon a dwarfish thief.*

Macbeth replies:

> *I will not be afraid of death and bane,*
>
> *Till Birnam Forest come to Dunsinane.*

Repeat the activity from Episode 1.3: choose whether to stay with the bloody butcher (Macbeth) or the brand new hope (Malcolm).

QUESTIONS

EARLY SKILLS	LATER SKILLS
Where is Macbeth?	
Where is Malcolm?	
Who is the King?	
	Who wants to be King?
What is Malcolm going to do?	
	Macbeth thinks he is safe. Why? Do you think he is safe?
	How does Macbeth feel?
	How does Malcolm feel?

Macbeth *thinks* he is safe because the witches have *said* that he will not be harmed until the wood moves. And woods don't move, do they?

SOCIAL COGNITION

Foundation Skills

Affect	Imitation.
Desire	Attention to agents. Goal-directed behaviour. Expression of wants.
Belief	Gaze monitoring.
Imagination	Role-play conventions.

Early Skills

Desire	Expression of desire, choice and intent. Awareness of intents of others. Desire vocabulary.
Belief	Naming.
Imagination	Role play. Figurative language.

Later Skills

Affect   Recognition of feelings of others.

Desire   Recognition of intentions of others. Intention/action connection. Explanations.

Belief   Recognition of beliefs of others. Perception-belief/knowledge connection. Explanations. Mental-state vocabulary.

Imagination   Role adoption. Figurative language.

7.4. Birnam Wood

Macbeth and his followers are at one end of the room, Malcolm and his followers at the other. Malcolm's followers hold branches; or you might tie them to wheelchairs, giving the impression that the wood is moving. Encourage students to vocalise, waving their tree branches as they approach.

Macbeth	*I will not be afraid of death and bane*
	Till Birnam Forest come to Dunsinane.
Watchman	*As I did stand my watch upon the hill*
	I looked toward Birnam, and anon methought
	The wood began to move.

Macbeth and his followers turn their backs, and Malcolm and his followers creep up on them. When Macbeth turns round, the wood must freeze.

The watchman says: 'The wood is moving!'

Macbeth says: 'Oh no it isn't!'

The army says: 'Oh yes it is!'

QUESTIONS

EARLY SKILLS	LATER SKILLS
What does Macbeth see?	
	What does he think is happening?
	Is the wood really moving?
	How does Macbeth feel?
	How does Malcolm feel?

At the end, Macbeth and his followers stand in the middle of a circle, and are converged on by the 'wood'. The crown is taken off Macbeth and put onto Malcolm.

SOCIAL COGNITION

Foundation Skills

Affect	Affective responses. Imitation. Situation/feeling connection.
Desire	Attention to agents. Goal-directed behaviour. Teasing (passive).

Belief	Attention to objects. Mutual gaze. Joint attention. Gaze monitoring. Declaratives. Teasing (active).
Imagination	Object exploration and manipulation. Play with sounds/movement. Role-play conventions.

Early Skills

Affect	Awareness of feelings. Situation/feeling connection. Stock reactions. Basic emotion vocabulary.
Belief	Naming. Perspective taking – recognition of what others see. Perception vocabulary. Belief vocabulary.
Imagination	Symbolic use of objects. Role play.

Later Skills

Affect	Recognition of feelings of others. Psychological causality.
Belief	Appearance/reality distinction. Recognition of beliefs of others. Mental-state vocabulary. Perception-belief/knowledge connection. Explanations. False belief. False belief vocabulary.
Imagination	Role adoption. Imagination vocabulary.

7.5. Out, Out, Brief Candle

Light a candle, or switch on a torch. Everyone sits quietly and listens to Macbeth's speech.

> *Tomorrow and tomorrow and tomorrow*
>
> *Creeps in this petty pace from day to day*
>
> *To the last syllable of recorded time;*
>
> *And all our yesterdays have lighted fools*
>
> *The way to dusty death. Out, out, brief candle!*
>
> *Life's but a walking shadow, a poor player*
>
> *That struts and frets his hour upon the stage*
>
> *And then is heard no more. It is a tale*
>
> *Told by an idiot, full of sound and fury,*
>
> *Signifying nothing.*

Blow out the candle – switch off the torch, so that there is darkness.

Alternative: Have one student or staff member move slowly behind a backlit curtain, projecting a shadow, from one side to the other.

SOCIAL COGNITION

Foundation Skills

Affect	Affective responses. Expressing feelings – sadness.
Belief	Attention to objects/patterns.
Imagination	Sensory images.

Early Skills

Affect	Awareness of feelings. Situation/feeling connection. Basic emotion vocabulary.
Imagination	Figurative language.

Later Skills

Affect	Recognition of feelings of others.
Imagination	Figurative language.

7.6. Kingdom's Pearl

Bring up the lights, and bow and clap to welcome the new King, Malcolm.

> *Hail King of Scotland!*

Put all the daggers, swords and armour into a wastebin, to signify that we are now at peace.

> *I see thee compassed as thy kingdom's pearl.*

This image of peace and purity recalls Macbeth's reference to *mine eternal jewel Given to the common enemy of man.* Create an orb or giant pearl (papier mâché, painted with luminous paint), or blow large, iridescent bubbles for students to reach towards, as they reached before to the crown. Malcolm can walk around the circle with the orb or bubbles.

Celebrate the new coronation with a feast, passing cups around to gentle, happy music and singing, to end on a calm, upbeat note. Using real food and drink here will encourage expression of wants.

QUESTIONS

EARLY SKILLS	LATER SKILLS
What are these? (Daggers) Do we need them? (No) What are these? (Goblets/cups) Do we need them? (Yes)	Why don't we need our daggers any more?
Who is the King now?	Do you think everyone is happy or sad? Why?

SOCIAL COGNITION

Foundation Skills

Affect	Affective responses. Imitation. Expressing feelings.
Desire	Attention to agents. Expression of wants.
Belief	Attention to events.
Imagination	Play with sound (singing). Object gestures. Role-play conventions.

Early Skills

Affect	Awareness of feelings. Situation/feeling connection. Stock reactions. Basic emotion vocabulary.
Desire	Expression of desires. Awareness of intents of others. Desire vocabulary.
Belief	Naming. Belief vocabulary.
Imagination	Pretend actions. Role play.

Later Skills

Affect	Recognition of feelings of others. Psychological causality.
Imagination	Role adoption.

James Kealy

Chapter 4

Macbeth in Mind in Practice

The following examples of workshops which have used the material in this book should not be regarded as systematic trials or pilots. Rather, they illustrate some different ways of using the resource with a wide range of students that we undertook at different stages of the writing. We were often very unsure whether the ideas we had discussed would work in practice with the students in question, and were surprised and excited by the outcomes on many occasions.

Students with Moderate Learning Difficulties

This was the first workshop we ever did on *Macbeth*, with a large group of pupils in an MLD school. They had studied the play beforehand, and made some superb props – a castle façade and trees – and costumes. The pupils sat in a semicircle, and we acted the play for and with them, inviting different pupils to take on the key roles in each scene. They were extremely attentive, and joined in with enthusiasm. For example, I was narrating the story at the point after the murder, and said 'When suddenly…' and paused. One of the pupils spontaneously and unexpectedly knocked loudly three times on a wooden bench – clearly having remembered what happened next. The effect was truly electrifying. Another pupil was showing some very autistic behaviours, wandering on and off the acting space, twiddling, and being apparently totally disengaged. We were playing the game in which groups suggest night noises to accompany Macbeth's advance to the King's room. Her group was the last I approached, and to my astonishment, she looked straight at me and produced an unearthly mewing sound, like a cat – which of course we adopted as the sound for her group.

Students with Autism

A half-day drama workshop was held at a residential school for children with autistic spectrum disorders. Again, a considerable amount of preparation had been done by staff, who were very skilled at using drama with the children. At the end we gathered round a flip chart to tell the story. There were seven pupils in the group, aged between 12 and 18. We put the story together through questions from staff (in italics) and contributions from the pupils, with a gifted art teacher drawing and writing on the flip chart. The 'cast' in the workshop was as follows:

Graham	Macbeth
Des	Cawdor
Alex	Malcolm
Matthew	Duncan
Jerrard	Guard
Patrick and **Steve**	Witches

Graham   That's olden days. About a thousand years ago. The King was Duncan. Macbeth and Cawdor.

And what did Cawdor do?

Des   Take the crown.

Patrick   We don't do this in real life. Just pretend.

Graham   But he lost the fight.

Alex   And he got sent to prison.

Graham   I got the silver crown.

Whose was it?

Graham   Cawdor's.

Macbeth was on his way home. What happened then?

Graham   And he saw three witches. Meet again.

When shall we three meet again? What did they show Macbeth?

Graham   Three crowns. Bronze, silver, gold.

And then what happened?

Graham   He wented back home to see Lady Macbeth.

Alex   And Lady Macbeth was pleased to see him. And they worked out how to kill him.

That's right. And what did they say? My dearest love, Duncan comes here tonight. And when goes hence?

Alex   Tomorrow ...

That's right, Tomorrow as he purposes. Oh never, shall sun that morrow see! So what happened when Duncan came to the castle?

Graham   And I was about to stab you with a knife, and they said 'Look behind you!' and I hid it behind my back.

Matthew   Macbeth (i.e. I saw Macbeth when I looked round).

And then what happened?

Graham   Went to sleep. And I killed him.

Who killed Duncan?

Matthew   Macbeth.

Graham   And they putted blood on the guards to make them think that they did it.

That's right. And then what did they hear?

Graham   Knock on the door.

Alex   Let me in, what's going on in there?

And when the people arrived, what did they see?

Matthew   Duncan's dead.

Graham   Looked for blood on the people's hands.

Alex   Macbeth became king.

Yes, and what did the people start to whisper?

Alex   Macbeth has murdered sleep.

Graham   I killed all of them.

So then, Macbeth went to visit the witches to find out what would happen

Graham   Making a magic spell for me to appear. They said, when you see the wood moving, you're in trouble.

Des   Hubble, bubble, toilet trouble.

(Explanation follows about the difference between toil and toilet).

What did the witches put in the cauldron?

Matthew   A dead finger.

Alex   An eye of newt.

Patrick   A snake.

Graham   A dead hand.

Jerrard   Bat.

Alex   Frog's legs.

Des   A sweet ... (*he had admired the colours of the plastic snake*). A
snake.

Right, so then Malcolm got all his friends together, and what did he do?

Alex   I led them towards the castle, and we all had woods, and we
crouched down and then we surrounded them.

And what were you doing in the castle, Graham, while this was happening?

Graham   Having a drink. Turned round, and then the wood stopped.
They was people attacking our castle to let Malcolm
become King.

And then everyone was happy. Why were they happy that Macbeth was dead?

Alex Because Macbeth killed Duncan.

We then put a poem together about Macbeth. Words in italics were contributed by staff.

How shall we start our poem?

Des   Hubble, bubble, toilet trouble.

Fire burn and cauldron bubble.

Night noises.

Alex   As Macbeth walks through.

Vampires.

Des   Ha ha ha.

Alex   Screeching doors screech here and there.

Patrick   There's an owl.

Too-whit too-whoo!

Alex   Macbeth draws closer.

As wolves howl.

Patrick   Wind.

Blows and whistles, whew.

As Macbeth is killing sleep.

Alex   Macbeth is King and here comes trouble.

Des   Knock on the door! Move it on the double!

So the finished poem looks like this:

> *Hubble, bubble, toil and trouble*
> *Fire burn and cauldron bubble.*
> *Night noises as Macbeth walks through.*
> *Vampires — ha ha ha*
> *Sceeching doors screech here and there*
> *There's an owl — too-whit too-whoo*
> *Macbeth draws closer*
> *As wolves howl.*
> *Wind blows and whistles, whew.*
> *As Macbeth is killing sleep.*
> *Macbeth is King, and here comes trouble.*
> *Knock on the door! Move it on the double!*
> *Hubble, bubble, toil and trouble*
> *Fire burn and cauldron bubble.*

The teachers involved in this workshop felt that the quality of language and understanding of concepts revealed by the children was much greater than they would have expected. The power of the story seemed to grip them, so much so that Alex, who normally hated role playing and refused to wear costume, kept Malcolm's golden crown on throughout the creative writing session, and finally brought it back at lunchtime, saying 'I s'pose I'd better give this back now.'

The recall showed by the students indicates that Graham and Alex had grasped the sequence of events, and something of the characters' motivation. Des and Alex recalled extracts from the text as well. Even Matthew, who was quite silent during the discussion, remembered exactly what had happened to him in role, and who was responsible. The discussion also shows how the events stimulate the use of mental-state vocabulary, and reference to the goals and intentions of protagonists.

The poem which we created in a very impromptu way shows appreciation of the rhythms and sounds of Shakespeare's language; the recall of the game 'Night Noises' lead to several rhymes within the text. The children's responses illustrate the attraction that poetic language can have for some autistic children. Des, who contributed the couplets, often uses snatches of remembered conversation to communicate. Rich language paired with body movement, natural gesture and sign seemed to the teachers to free up the children's imagination, whereas an insistence on simplified language paired with key word signs would have been constricting.

Students with Severe and Profound Learning Difficulties

Sessions were carried out weekly for approximately 45 minutes over an eight-week period with 12 students aged between 11 and 16, two teachers and four classroom assistants. Up to ten students could be considered to be functioning within the range of profound and multiple learning difficulties. All students had significant additional disabilities. Seven were non-ambulant, and only one could walk independently. Six students had known visual impairments, ten had epilepsy (three having frequent and severe fits); one student was autistic and there were two girls with Retts Syndrome. Language abilities varied among the group. Six students functioned at a pre-intentional level of communication. Four students could be said to show consistent and reliable responses to everyday language in familiar situations. Two students had a repertoire of distinct vocalisations and gestures, one had a small vocabulary of words and signs, and one was hyperverbal and echolalic.

The sessions were conducted at an early stage of the development of the resource, and were experimental, being designed to test out what would work with a group of very disabled students. It was apparent that although not all students engaged consistently with the activities, the sessions were enjoyed. The student with echolalia has a real love of the sound of language, and picked up several Shakespearian turns of phrase. 'Fair is foul and foul is fair?' was her way of asking 'Are we doing *Macbeth* today?' The student with autism, who finds it hard to participate in a group, amazed us by definitely moving to sit with the King in the activity where participants were asked to choose sides. Later, when confronted with a masked face in the game 'Shadow Play', he stayed still and looked intently into my eyes. One student, who again found it hard to join in a group, and often disengages, was elected to play Duncan's sleeping guard. At the point where everyone is asked if their hands are clean, and who killed Duncan, she could be seen raising her hands in the air and shaking her head, demonstrating that she can understand some language at a two-word level, and could participate appropriately in a group activity.

At the end of the project, the consensus was that the following outcomes had been observed:

Socialisation – interaction with different people in a bigger group and experience of a different kind of activity.

Emotions – excitement, enjoyment, surprise, engagement, reactive and imitative behaviour.

Focusing – directional looking.

Anticipation and recall – both of the session itself and within activities.

Toleration – of costumes, props, make-up.

Vocalisation – imitative and spontaneous

Staff felt that these aspects improved over time as students became more familiar with the programme. Staff participation was felt to be essential for students to become successfully involved.

Students with Severe Physical and Sensory Difficulties

The speech and language therapist and specialist teacher for visual impairment used the resource in a two-hour session once a week at a school for pupils with physical disabilities with a group of six students aged between 12 and 15, all functioning at an early stage of communication development. All needed objects of reference to understand events. All vocalised spontaneously, but only one student had any functional speech. Five had a significant visual impairment, so a great deal of use was made of multi-sensory input, including equipment such as the sound beam, resonance board, infinity light tunnel and bubble tube. A simple record form was used in each session (see Appendix 2), and several sessions were videoed. This was helpful for seeing responses that might have been missed at the time, and noting progress. The therapist reported that all the students made some progress in both the subject-based and the developmentally based learning objectives.

Subject-Based Objectives

All of the students seemed to enjoy the atmosphere, with several of them vocalising very loudly when they came into the room, which they would not usually do. Two showed some degree of anticipation and recall, with the one verbal student saying 'King!' as soon as she came into the room, and the other immediately reaching out towards the cauldron, which was always used at the start of each session.

Developmentally Based Objectives

All of the students began to imitate sounds, which they did not do regularly before. Imitating action and facial expressions was not possible, owing to their visual impairments. The one student who had functional vision did look at the relevant characters in the play, when given auditory and visual cues to do so, and developed the ability to follow the gaze of others. This was a student with severe epilepsy and some autistic features, for whom joint attention had proved very difficult to establish. These sessions seemed to prove a turning point, and he is now developing useful interactions with others. Several students demonstrated appropriate use of objects, for example reaching out for the crown and putting it on their heads. The students showed different reactions to positive and scary atmospheres – when excited in the battle scenes, they would vocalise loudly, clap, press switches enthusiastically. In the scenes with the witches, when the soundbeam was used in a minor key, the tactile experiences were pretend cobwebs, and the infinity tunnel was used, the students became very quiet, still and attentive.

The therapist wrote: 'We all felt that both the students and us had really "experienced" at least some of the key elements of *Macbeth*, and we'd had great fun doing it!'

This is me as a
soldier in

macbeth

Appendix I

SKILLS OF SOCIAL COGNITION:
Operational Definitions

FOUNDATION SKILL	BEHAVIOURAL EVIDENCE	ACTIVITIES[1]
Affect	**Affect is defined as a marked behavioural state – either positive, negative or neutral. Neutral affect is often associated with attention.**	
Affective responses	Smiling, laughing, stilling, grimacing, gaze avoidance, eye widening, pausing, pushing away, turning towards, contingent vocalisation, synchronous movements.	1.1; 1.3; 1.4; 2.1; 2.5; 2.6; 3.1; 3.2; 3.3; 4.1; 4.2; 4.3; 4.4; 4.5; 5.1; 5.2; 5.3; 5.4; 6.1; 7.1; 7.2; 7.4; 7.5; 7.6.
Imitation	Immediate or slightly delayed repetition of the action, sound, facial expression or body posture of another person.	1.1; 1.3; 1.4; 2.1; 2.2; 2.5; 2.6; 3.3; 4.1; 4.2; 4.3; 4.4; 4.5; 5.1; 5.2; 5.3; 5.4; 6.1; 6.2; 7.1; 7.4; 7.6.
Expressing feelings	Signs of definite and consistent affective responses that can be conventionally recognised as positive or negative, associated with particular events.	1.1; 2.1; 2.5; 2.6; 3.3; 4.1; 4.2; 4.3; 4.4; 5.1; 5.3; 5.4; 6.1; 7.1; 7.2; 7.4; 7.5; 7.6.
Desire	**Desire is defined as the expression of wants, intentions to gain something or to reach a goal.**	
Attention to agents	Signs of definite attention to a person who is taking an active role (i.e. is an agent) – tracking, scanning, watching, touching. Anticipatory behaviour.	1.1; 1.2; 1.3; 1.4; 2.1; 2.2; 2.3; 2.5; 2.6; 3.1; 3.3; 4.1; 4.2; 4.3; 4.4; 4.5; 5.2; 5.3; 5.4; 6.2; 6.6; 7.1; 7.2; 7.3; 7.4; 7.6.

1. The numbers in this column refer to the Episode subsections in Chapter 3.

Goal-directed behaviour	Purposeful attempts to achieve particular ends, showing some appreciation of cause and effect: means-end behaviour, e.g. pulling a string to get an object; purposive movement, e.g. reaching, moving towards a particular place; altering a behaviour which has been unsuccessful, e.g. feeling inside a container, then shaking it to retrieve an object; persistent behaviour which stops when the end has been achieved; signs of frustration if the goal is not met, or satisfaction if it is.	1.1; 1.2; 1.3; 1.4; 2.1; 2.2; 3.1; 3.2; 4.2; 4.3; 4.5; 5.3; 6.1; 7.3; 7.4.
Pre-verbal expression of wants	Reaching, insistent vocalisation, gaze or touch alternation between a person and an object to signal a request.	1.2; 1.3; 2.2; 3.2; 6.1; 7.3; 7.6.
Teasing (passive)	Definite reactions such as laughing, looking away, raising hands when teased through tone of voice or action, e.g. when an object is offered and then withdrawn. The reaction suggests that there is recognition that this is a game rather than for real e.g. giggles rather than frustration.	1.3; 2.3; 2.6; 3.2; 3.3; 5.1; 5.4; 6.6.
Belief	**Belief is defined as a set of expectations about how the world functions, and how others behave, built on perceptions of experiences, and attention.**	
Attention to objects/sounds/events	Sustained gaze at or exploration of objects/patterns, indicating interest. Anticipatory behaviour. Location of sounds or sights. Evidence of perception of novelty, e.g. surprise through eye widening when a different object is introduced into a game or routine, or when something happens suddenly.	1.2; 1.3; 2.2; 2.3; 2.4; 2.6; 3.2; 3.4; 4.2; 4.3; 6.1; 6.3; 6.4; 7.2; 7.4; 7.5; 7.6. 2.1; 3.1; 3.3; 4.1; 4.3; 6.1; 6.2; 7.1; 7.4. 2.6; 4.4; 5.1; 5.3; 5.4; 6.1; 6.2; 6.4; 6.6; 7.1; 7.4.
Mutual gaze	Intense gaze at the face of another person – eye contact, or interaction through touch.	1.1; 1.3; 2.2; 2.5; 2.6; 3.3; 5.1; 5.2; 5.3; 5.4; 6.5; 6.6; 7.2; 7.4.

Joint attention	Evidence of awareness of a shared focus, which may be carer-directed at first: two people explore an object or event, looking between the object and each other, adjusting body movement, touching alternately the object and the other person.	1.2; 1.3; 2.1; 2.2; 2.3; 2.5; 2.6; 3.2; 3.3; 3.4; 4.2; 4.3; 4.4; 4.5; 5.1; 5.3; 5.4; 6.1; 6.2; 6.3; 6.4; 6.5; 6.6; 7.1; 7.2; 7.4.
Gaze monitoring	An advance on mutual gaze and joint attention. Tracking of another person's line of vision, point or movement – looking where someone else is looking, follow my leader behaviour, turning head to see where someone is going.	1.2; 1.3; 1.4; 2.1; 2.2; 2.5; 2.6; 3.3; 3.4; 4.2; 4.3; 4.4; 4.5; 5.1; 5.3; 5.4; 6.1; 6.2; 6.4; 6.6; 7.3; 7.4.
Declaratives	Behaviour which is directed to attracting the attention or interest of another person to something in the world – to say, 'Look at this' rather than 'I want this' e.g. offering an object, pointing to an object and looking at another person, vocalisation which seems to indicate 'Here I am, look at me'.	1.1; 1.2; 2.1; 2.2; 2.6; 3.3; 3.4; 4.3; 4.4; 5.1; 5.3; 5.4; 6.1; 6.2; 6.4; 6.6; 7.4.
Teasing (active)	Intentional teasing of another person, and checking of their reactions, e.g. withholding objects; refusing to say hello; starting an action then stopping it; acting as 'it' in games such as Grandmother's Footsteps; deliberately offering something you know will be rejected, as a game.	1.3; 2.2; 3.3; 5.1; 5.4; 6.1; 6.6; 7.4.
Imagination	**Imaginative behaviour involves the construction of an alternative representation from that which is immediately present. The roots of imaginative behaviour lie in play and exploration of the possibilities involved in objects and actions.**	
Sensory images	Experience of strong visual/auditory/tactile contrastive experiences that may lead to the formation of images in the memory, and which have symbolic power, e.g. light and dark; stickiness on the hands.	1.3; 2.1; 2.2; 2.6; 3.1; 3.2; 3.4; 4.1; 4.2; 4.3; 5.3; 6.1; 6.2; 6.3; 6.4; 6.5; 7.1; 7.2; 7.5.
Object exploration and manipulation	Touching, holding, shaking, dropping, mouthing, pushing and pulling.	2.2; 2.3; 2.4; 2.6; 3.1; 3.3; 3.4; 6.1; 6.4; 7.4.

Object gestures	Functional use of objects out of the usual context – putting brush to hair, cup to mouth, phone to ear.	2.3; 2.4; 3.3; 5.4; 7.6.
Play with sounds, movements and handshapes	Vocal or manual babble – playing with the elements of language for its own sake (babies who sign sometimes play with handshapes, looking intently at them). Joining in with rhythmic sounds or movements.	1.3; 1.4; 2.1; 2.2; 4.2; 6.1; 6.4; 7.1; 7.2; 7.4; 7.6.
Role-play conventions	Toleration, or evidence of expectation/ understanding of role-play conventions, e.g. of coming together in a circle, wearing costumes, holding props.	1.1; 1.2; 1.3; 1.4; 2.1; 2.2; 2.5; 3.3; 4.2; 4.3; 4.4; 4.5; 5.1; 5.3; 5.4; 6.1; 7.3; 7.4; 7.6.
EARLY SKILLS	**BEHAVIOURAL EVIDENCE**	**ACTIVITIES**
Affect	**Affect is defined as a marked behavioural state - either positive, negative or neutral.**	
Awareness of feelings	Empathetic reactions, e.g. looking sad when someone else is sad or reaching to touch them. Imitating facial expressions appropriately.	1.3; 1.4; 2.5; 2.6; 3.3; 4.1; 4.2; 4.3; 4.4; 5.1; 5.2; 5.3; 5.4; 6.1; 7.1; 7.2; 7.4; 7.5; 7.6.
Situation/feeling connection	Showing consistent appropriate response to a situation in the narrative, e.g. getting excited in the battle scene, falling quiet during the murder.	1.1; 1.3; 1.4; 2.5; 3.3; 4.1; 4.2; 4.3; 4.4; 5.1; 5.3; 5.4; 6.1; 7.1; 7.2; 7.4; 7.5; 7.6.
Stock reactions to characters and situations	Shows understanding of characters who are 'good', 'bad' 'royal', e.g. hissing or booing the villain, shouting hooray for the hero, 'ahh bless' for lovers, bowing for King, shuddering when 'ghost' or witches appear.	1.1; 1.3; 3.1; 3.3; 4.2; 4.3; 4.4; 4.5; 5.1; 5.3; 5.4; 6.1; 7.4; 7.6.
Basic emotion vocabulary	Shows understanding of emotion words, e.g. by pointing to someone who is 'happy' 'sad'. Produce different facial and body expressions when asked to demonstrate feelings. Use of basic emotion words such as: 'happy', 'sad', 'angry', 'frightened', 'tired', 'hungry'.	1.1; 1.4; 2.6; 3.3; 4.1; 4.2; 4.4; 5.2; 5.3; 7.2; 7.4; 7.5; 7.6.

Desire	**Desire is defined as the expression of wants and intentions to gain something or reach a goal.**	
Expression of desire and intent	Expressing definite preferences and making choices. Use and understanding of desire vocabulary.	1.2; 1.3; 2.2; 3.2; 3.3; 4.5; 5.1; 6.1; 7.3; 7.6.
Awareness of wants of others	Showing awareness of wants/needs of others, e.g. passing the cauldron/goblet to the next person without prompting; opening the door as someone knocks on it. Ability to identify a person who wants something, with support and prompting – e.g. can point to Macbeth when asked 'Who wants the crown?'	1.2; 1.3; 1.4; 2.2; 2.3; 2.5; 3.2; 3.3; 4.5; 6.1; 7.3; 7.6.
Cause and effect	Clear evidence of understanding of connection between events and consequences, e.g. pointing to Macbeth when asked who killed the King, pushing something and laughing when it falls over.	1.4; 4.3; 4.4; 5.1; 5.3.
Desire vocabulary	'Yes', 'no', 'want', 'give me', 'like', 'don't like', 'more', 'again', 'will', 'won't'.	1.2; 1.3; 2.2; 3.2; 6.1; 7.3; 7.6.
Belief	**Belief is defined as a set of expectations about how the world functions, and how others behave.**	
Naming and description	Identifying and/or naming objects, events and people; understanding/using simple adjectives to describe people, places and things.	1.1; 1.2; 1.3; 2.1; 2.2; 2.3; 2.4; 3.1; 3.4; 4.2; 5.1; 5.3; 5.4; 6.1; 6.2; 6.4; 6.6; 7.1; 7.3; 7.6.
Recognition of actions of self and others	Identify what self or others are doing or have done.	1.4; 2.4; 3.3; 4.1; 4.3; 4.4; 5.1; 5.3; 6.1; 7.1; 7.2; 7.3.
Perspective taking – recognition of one's own perspective	Responding appropriately when asked 'What are you looking at?' 'what will you do next?'; 'what can you hear?'	1.3; 2.1; 3.1; 3.3; 3.4; 4.2; 4.4; 5.4; 6.4; 6.6; 7.1; 7.4.

Perspective taking – recognition of what others perceive	Identifying what others are looking at, saying, touching, tasting, hearing. Taking account of perspective of others, e.g. turning picture round to show you; stopping moving when Macbeth turns and points.	1.2; 1.3; 2.1; 2.4; 3.1; 3.3; 3.4; 4.1; 4.2; 4.4; 4.5; 5.1; 5.2; 5.3; 5.4; 6.6; 7.1; 7.4.
Perception vocabulary: sensory perception	'See', 'hear', 'touch', 'listen', 'watch', 'smell', 'taste', 'move', 'say'.	1.2; 2.5; 3.1; 3.3; 3.4; 4.2; 4.4; 4.5; 5.1; 5.2; 5.3; 5.4; 6.6; 7.1; 7.4.
Belief vocabulary	Words which are associated with the existence of things and people: 'gone', 'here', 'there', 'yes', 'no' used to confirm or deny the truth or existence of something.	2.1; 2.2; 3.4; 4.4; 5.3; 6.6; 7.4; 7.6.
Imagination	**Imaginative behaviour involves the construction of an alternative representation to that which is immediately present.**	
Symbolic use of objects & object substitution	Use toy/pretend objects to perform action eg. stab with dagger, hide behind cardboard tree. Use one object as though it were another eg. use drumstick as witch's wand; put bricks on plate for pretend food.	2.3; 2.4; 2.6; 3.2; 3.3; 3.4; 6.1;
Pretend actions and use of imaginary objects	Carrying out an action in an imaginative context, e.g. pretending to wash and dry hands; using imaginary dagger or cup.	1.1; 2.4; 2.6; 3.4; 4.2; 4.4; 5.4; 6.1; 7.6.
Role play	Acting appropriately in role (imitation or spontaneous), e.g. performing conjuring action when acting as witch, bowing to the King.	1.1; 1.2; 1.3; 1.4; 2.1; 2.2; 2.4; 2.5; 3.1; 3.3; 4.4; 4.5; 5.1; 5.2; 5.3; 5.4; 6.1; 6.2; 7.2; 7.3; 7.6.
Figurative language	Showing awareness or interest in imaginative language, e.g. by repeating liked phrases.	2.1; 2.3; 2.6; 3.1; 3.2; 3.4; 4.1; 5.2; 5.3; 6.1; 6.3; 6.4; 7.1; 7.2; 7.3; 7.5.
	Perceiving associations between things or events, e.g. daggers and teeth are sharp; roses and hearts are red.	2.3; 2.6; 3.2; 5.3.
	Classifying objects into categories based on perceptual or other shared features.	

LATER SKILLS	BEHAVIOURAL EVIDENCE	ACTIVITIES
Affect	**Affect is defined as a marked behavioural state – either positive, negative or neutral.**	
Recognition of feelings of others	Identifying and discussing how people feel.	1.3; 1.4; 2.3; 2.5; 2.6; 3.2; 3.3; 4.1; 4.4; 5.1; 5.2; 5.3; 5.4; 7.1; 7.2; 7.3; 7.4; 7.5; 7.6.
Psychological causality: desire-emotion, belief/knowledge-emotion	Understanding the connection between: wants and feelings, e.g. Macbeth feels jealous because he wants the crown; beliefs and feelings, e.g. Banquo feels worried because he thinks Macbeth has killed Duncan; actions/events and feelings, e.g. Lady Macbeth feels guilty because she killed Duncan; Malcolm is happy and triumphant because he is King, and there is no more war.	1.2; 1.4; 2.3; 2.6; 3.2; 3.3; 4.1; 4.4; 5.1; 5.2; 5.3; 5.4; 7.1; 7.2; 7.4; 7.6.
Mixed feelings	Understanding that people can have conflicting or different feelings, e.g. both happy and sad at the same time .	1.3; 2.3; 2.6; 3.2.
Complex emotion vocabulary	'Jealous', 'guilty', 'anxious', 'suspicious', 'proud', 'triumphant', 'ambitious', 'honest', 'truthful', 'modest', 'shy', 'excited'.	1.2; 1.4; 2.3; 2.6; 3.2; 5.1; 5.2; 5.4; 7.1; 7.2; 7.6.
Desire	**Desire is defined as the expression of wants, intentions to gain something to supply a need.**	
Recognition of intentions of others	Understanding that other people have intentions that are distinct from one's own, e.g. Macbeth is planning to kill the King; Banquo is planning to go hunting before dinner.	1.2; 1.3; 1.4; 2.2; 2.3; 2.4; 2.5; 3.3; 4.1; 4.4; 5.1; 5.2; 5.3; 7.3.
Intention/action connection	Understanding that intentions lead to actions, e.g. Macbeth wants the crown so he will kill Duncan.	1.3; 2.3; 3.2; 3.3; 4.1; 4.4; 5.1; 5.2; 5.3; 7.3.

Skill	Definition	
Explanations	Can provide or indicate explanations of events and behaviour which relate intentions to consequences. Can use and understand terms such as: 'because' 'if' 'so' 'then'.	1.2; 1.3; 2.4; 3.2; 3.3; 4.1; 4.3; 5.2; 7.3.
Belief	**Belief is defined as a set of expectations about how the world functions, and how others behave.**	
Recognition of beliefs of others	Understanding that other people have beliefs that are distinct from one's own, e.g. Duncan thinks Macbeth is a friend, we think he is not.	1.2; 1.3; 1.4; 2.3; 2.4; 2.6; 3.1; 3.3; 3.4; 4.2; 4.4; 4.5; 5.2; 5.3; 5.4; 7.3; 7.4.
Perception-belief/knowledge connection	Understanding that perception leads to knowledge and belief, e.g. Duncan sees the 'pleasant seat' of the castle and believes it to be welcoming; the blood on the faces of the guards leads others to think that they have killed Duncan.	1.2; 1.3; 2.6; 3.1; 3.3; 3.4; 4.4; 5.4; 6.6; 7.3; 7.4.
Appearance/reality distinction	Understanding that what people say or do may be different from what they think or feel. Lady Macbeth says welcome to Duncan, but is thinking she will kill him. Understand that events may or may not 'really' happen, e.g. Banquo is not really at the feast; the wood is not really moving. Understanding and being able to explain that appearances may be deceptive, e.g. you think you see a dagger, but it is really a stick; you think you see a wood moving, but the people are moving, not the trees.	1.2; 1.3; 1.4; 2.6; 3.1; 3.3; 3.4; 4.4; 4.5; 5.1; 5.2; 5.4; 7.4.
Explanations	Ability to provide or indicate explanations of events and behaviour which relate beliefs to consequences; understanding connection between evidence and events, e.g. Macbeth has blood on his hands, which means he has killed the King; tracks on the floor point to where someone has gone.	2.1; 3.1; 3.3; 4.3; 4.4; 5.3; 5.4; 6.6; 7.3.
Mental-state vocabulary	'Think', 'know', 'believe', 'understand', 'feel', 'guess', 'hope', 'wish', 'expect'.	1.3; 1.4; 2.1; 2.3; 2.4; 2.6; 3.1; 3.3; 3.4; 4.2; 4.4; 4.5; 5.1; 5.2; 5.3; 5.4; 7.3.

False belief	Understanding that people can believe things that are not true. Understanding concepts of trick and pretence.	1.2; 1.3; 2.6; 3.1; 3.3; 3.4; 4.4; 5.1; 5.2; 7.4.
False belief vocabulary	'Pretend', 'deceive', 'lie', 'trick', 'tease', 'trust', 'betray', 'truth', 'joke'.	1.2; 1.3; 1.4; 2.6; 3.1; 3.3; 4.4; 5.1; 5.2; 7.4.
Imagination	**Imaginative behaviour involves the construction of an alternative representation from that which is immediately present.**	
Role adoption and imaginative play	Ability to sustain and develop a role through appropriate actions and dialogue. Taking part in sustained fantasy play, e.g. using monologues describing pretend actions.	1.2; 1.3; 2.1; 2.2; 2.4; 3.3; 3.4; 4.1; 4.2; 4.3; 4.4; 4.5; 5.1; 5.2; 5.3; 5.4; 6.1; 7.3; 7.4; 7.6.
	Suggesting imaginative activities or developments to a plot, e.g. suggesting who should be King instead of Macbeth.	2.4; 4.2; 4.5; 5.4; 6.1; 6.2.
Recognition of imaginative states	Understand notions of mental reality such as play, dreams and imagination, e.g. describeing a dream.	3.4; 4.1; 5.4; 7.1; 7.2.
Imagination vocabulary	'pretend', 'dream', 'imagine', 'make up', 'play'.	2.6; 3.4; 4.1; 5.4; 7.1; 7.2.
Figurative language	Ability to generate similes and metaphors; explain the basis of simile and metaphor; use language figuratively, e.g. in jokes, puns, poetry. Understanding non-literal use of language, e.g. in figures of speech, sarcasm, irony.	2.6; 3.1; 3.4; 4.1; 5.3; 6.1; 6.3; 7.3; 7.5.

Appendix 2

Communication record sheet

Communication Record Sheet

Name									Date	
What meanings are communicated	How meaning is communicated									Comments
	Body Orientation	Using Hands	Facial Expression	Eye Gaze	Vocalisation	Using Objects	Gesture	Pointing	Speech	Level 1/2/3/4
Focusing attention										
Vocalisations in response										
Initiation										
Interaction with peers										
Ability to copy with different situations										

References

Astington, J. W. and Gopnik, A. (1988) 'Knowing you've changed your mind: Children's understanding of representational change.' In J. W. Astington, P. L. Harris and D. R. Olson (eds) *Developing Theories of Mind*. Cambridge: CUP.

Baron-Cohen, S. and Ring, H. (1994) 'A model of the mindreading system: Neuropsychological and neurobiological perspectives.' In C. Lewis and P. Mitchell (eds) *Children's Early Understanding of Mind: Origins and Development*. Hove: LEA.

Bolton, G. (1986) *Selected Writings on Drama and Education*. London and New York: Longman.

Bowerman, M. (1978) 'The acquisition of word meaning: An investigation into some current conflicts.' In N. Waterson and C. Snow (eds) *The Development of Communication*. Chichester: Wiley.

Bowler, D. and Strom, E. (1998) 'Elicitation of first order theory of mind in children with autism.' *Autism: The International Journal of Research and Practice 2*.

Butterworth, G. (1991) 'The ontogeny and phylogeny of joint visual attention.' In A. Whiten (ed) *Natural Theories of Mind: Evolution, Development and Simulation of Everyday Mindreading*. Oxford: Basil Blackwell.

Camaioni, L. (1992) 'Mind knowledge in infancy: the emergence of intentional communication.' *Early Development and Parenting 1*, 15–22.

Charman, T. and Baron-Cohen, S. (1997) 'Brief report: Prompted pretend play in autism.' *Journal of Autism and Developmental Disorders 27*, 325–332.

Crystal, D. (1997) 'Language play and linguistic intervention.' *Child Language Teaching and Therapy 13*, 328–345.

Flavell, J. H., Everett, B. A., Croft, K. and Flavell, E.R. (1981) 'Young children's knowledge about visual perception: Further evidence for the Level 1–Level 2 distinction.' *Developmental Psychology 17*, 99–103.

Grove, N. and Park, K. (1996) *Odyssey Now*. London: Jessica Kingsley Publishers.

Haviland, J. M. and Lelwica, M. (1987) 'The induced affect response: 10-week old infants' responses to three emotion expressions.' *Developmental Psychology 23*, 97–104.

Howlin, P., Baron-Cohen, S. and Hadwin, J. (1999) *Teaching Children with Autism Theory of Mind: A Practical Guide*. Chicester: Wiley.

Jennings, S. (1986) *Creative Drama in Groupwork*. Bicester: Winslow Press.

Lakoff, G. and Johnson, M. (1980) *Metaphors We Live By*. Chicago: University of Chicago Press.

Lewis, V. and Boucher, J. (1988) 'Spontaneous, elicited and pretend play in relatively able autistic children. *British Journal of Developmental Psychology 6*, 325–339.

Libby, S., Powell, S., Messer, D. and Jordan, R. (1998) 'Spontaneous play in children with autism: A reappraisal.' *Journal of Autism and Developmental Disorders 28*, 487–497.

Mandler, J. (1992) 'How to build a baby II: Conceptual primitives.' *Psychological Review 99*, 4, 587–604.

Masur, E. F. (1983) 'Gestural development, dual-directional signalling and the transition to words.' *Journal of Psycholinguistic Research 12*, 93–109.

Meltzhoff, A. N. and Gopnik, A. (1993) 'The role of imitation in understanding persons and developing a theory of mind.' In S. Baron-Cohen, H. Tager-Flusberg and D. J. Cohen (eds) *Understanding Other Minds: Perspectives from Autism.* Oxford: OUP.

Nafstad, A. and Rodbroe, I. (1999) *Co-creating Communication: Perspectives on Diagnostic Education for Individuals Who are Congenitally Deafblind and Individuals Whose Impairments May have Similar Effects.* Dronninglund, Denmark: Forlage Nord-Press.

Park, K. (1995) 'Early theory of mind and the emergence of intentional communication in children with severe learning disabilities.' Paper delivered at the British Institute of Learning Disabilities Conference, Oxford.

Perez-Pereira, M. and Conti-Ramsden, G. (1999) *Language Development and Social Interaction in Blind Children.* Hove: Psychology Press.

Petitto, L. and Marentette, P. (1991) 'Babbling in the manual mode: Evidence for theontogeny of language.' *Science 251*, 1493–1496.

Poulin-Dubois, D. and Shultz, T. (1988) 'The development of the understanding of human behavior: from agency to intentionality.' In J. W. Astington, P. L. Harris and D. R. Olson (eds) *Developing Theories of Mind.* Cambridge: CUP.

Reddy, V. (1991) 'Playing with others' expectations: Teasing and mucking about in the first year.' In A. Whiten (ed) *Natural Theories of Mind: Evolution, Development and Simulation of Everyday Mindreading.* Oxford: Basil Blackwell.

Sherratt, D. (1999) 'The importance of play.' In G. Jones (ed) *Good Autism Practice.* Birmingham: University of Birmingham.

Stahmer, A. C. (1999) 'Using pivotal response training to facilitate appropriate play in children with autistic spectrum disorders.' *Child Language Teaching and Therapy 15*, 41–52.

Turner, M. (1996) *The Literary Mind: The Origins of Thought and Language.* Oxford: OUP.

Wellman, H. M. (1993) 'Early understanding of mind: The normal case.' In S. Baron-Cohen, H. Tager-Flusberg and D. J. Cohen (eds) *Understanding Other Minds: Perspectives from Autism.* Oxford: OUP.

Wolfberg, P. and Schuler, A. (1999) 'Fostering peer interaction, imaginative play and spontaneous language in children with autism.' *Child Language Teaching and Therapy 15*, 41–52.

Yirmaya, N., Pilowsky, T., Solomonica-Levi, D. and Shulman, C. (1999) 'Behaviour and theory of mind abilities in individuals with autism, Down Syndrome and mental retardation of unknown aetiology.' *Journal of Autism and Developmental Disorders 29*, 333–341.